trash
talk

"*Trash Talk*, by Jack Witt, is an insightful, eye-opening primer on the importance of self-awareness, followed by an awareness and acceptance of others. Using accessible metaphors, Mr. Witt manages to relate important, thought-provoking images that invite the reader to perceive themselves and others in an accurate, yet at the same time liberating manner.

The book manages to be entertaining yet meaningful as it gently allows the reader to examine themselves and others in a more loving manner. Mr. Witt's compassion and caring for others is evident in the book's pages, as is his wisdom gained from years of working with others."

—**J. Reid McKellar, Ph.D.,** *Clinical Psychologist*

"Engaging, unique and readable...Travel alongside Jack Witt in *Trash Talk* to gain vital navigation in an often disconnected and conflict-wrought world while also discovering insight and practical tools to build, repair, and strengthen relationships along the roadways of life."

—**Heidi S. Messner, M.A. Psychology,**
Regional Pastor & Author

Trash Talk is a useful and fun read – practical - yet nutrient filled and pivotal in providing clear and simple tools for enhancing self-awareness and revitalizing relationships. I found the weaving of foundational concepts into current societal trends to be a welcome and tempting reset for reorganizing and assessing current relationships. I look forward to reading what Jack writes in the future.

—Delrae Hansen Stayer, MA LMFT,

ISFC Program Director · Social Work Supervisor

J. CURTIS WITT

trash talk

HOW TO
Upgrade Your Self-Awareness
and Unclutter Your Relationships

Outside Insight Press

For my loving wife, Pamela
who brings out the best in me.
I'm truly grateful for all the miles
we've traveled together.
And for my ever-encouraging,
emotionally intelligent kids,
Jarred, Megan, and Katelyn.
With all my love

contents

1

preface

7

CHAPTER ONE

wanderlust

17

CHAPTER TWO

broken pieces of automobiles

27

CHAPTER THREE

cargo straps

41

CHAPTER FOUR

ice chest lids

53

CHAPTER FIVE

ladders

61

CHAPTER SIX

black rubber

69

CHAPTER SEVEN

broken furniture

77

CHAPTER EIGHT

hats

87

CHAPTER NINE

ordinary paper trash

95

CHAPTER TEN

life vests

103

CHAPTER ELEVEN

making peace with what is

117

CHAPTER TWELVE

adopt-my-highway

129

CHAPTER THIRTEEN

cleaned-up expectations

139

CHAPTER FOURTEEN

separating the debris

151

conclusion

157

end notes

preface

How long are those dashed lines on the road. . . you know, those painted broken lines that separate lanes of traffic on the highway? Most people guess two feet. They actually measure ten feet, spaced thirty to forty feet apart. The lines appear much smaller to us because of the speed at which our vehicles pass alongside them. Outside of guessed observations made at sixty or seventy miles per hour, to accurately know the length of broken white lines on the highway, you must believe what someone tells you about them (as I just did), or find out for yourself by pulling your car over, grabbing a tape measure and playing dodgeball with speeding vehicles.

Most of our estimations like size, scale, and age are based on quick impressions and guesses. I've (gratefully) had enough wisdom to keep myself from estimating people's weight, and I gave up on trying to guess people's age a long time ago because I was so horrible at it. Sadly, another exciting carnival career will have to be nixed from my bucket list.

Guestimates, however, are not confined to benign information like the length of white reflective stripes on a highway or the risky business of estimating a person's age and weight. We regularly form impressions and guesses about the motives, sincerity, and reasoning behind others' behavior. Sometimes we even attempt a quick guess at the root motivations driving our own actions. The problem is that this guessing happens mostly subconsciously and always at the fast highway-speed of life.

It would be helpful to notice how quickly our impressions become conclusions we hold without further questions or the search for better truth. I tend to think of them as drive-by assumptions. They harm us by keeping us blind to our true selves and contribute unnecessary damage to our personal relationships. I'm regularly concerned as I observe people who are basing their behaviors and significant decisions on impressions and quickly created assumptions. Certainly, others have carried that same concern for me.

I've been in the people-business for a long time. From serving as a minister at one end of my career to consulting and training on social-emotional development with multi-million-dollar corporations on the other, my work experience and education have consistently focused on helping people better understand themselves and others. A colleague once questioned me with a bit of surprise, "You actually like people, don't you?"

I do. What has helped me like people is giving up on attempts to make everyone be the way I think they should be. Appreciating who they are allows me to influence their development toward the best qualities they want for themselves and to enjoy them in that process.

You and every person in your circle of relationships are wonderfully complex. We do not comprehend the size and scale of the human soul when seen through quick glances at highway speeds. To move beyond drive-by assumptions you will need healthy self-insight and the ability to see other human beings accurately. Those abilities fall into the territory of Emotional Intelligence (EI). While your Intelligence Quotient (IQ) could predict your success in academic performance or the ability to master technical, mathematical, linguistic, or logical competencies, IQ has surprisingly little influence on how successful you are personally and even professionally.

As a colleague and I were leaving a particularly disastrous staff meeting a few years ago, she stopped in the hallway, threw her hands up in the air and asked, "How can that man be so brilliantly stupid?" I understood her frustration. The manager who had derailed the meeting was one of the most intelligent individuals we knew. His lack of self-awareness and inability to read and respond to social environments regularly obscured his intellectual brilliance and undermined his influence.

In a practical sense, Emotional Intelligence is the ability to recognize your own emotions and manage the way your feelings impact your interactions with others. If you subscribe to the idea that we place too much attention on feelings and everyone needs to just "buck up" and get on with doing what needs to be done, you are certainly entitled to hold that belief.

Before you slam the door on the subject however, you may want to know that the benefits of growing in Emotional Intelligence are massive. Over 70% of hiring managers say they value EI over IQ. Corporations understand that most people can be trained in the skills required to perform technical tasks, but if an employee can't communicate effectively, bond with others, show empathy, and manage their own emotions, they will tend to produce constant disruptions in the organization and impede collaboration.

The personal side of EI benefits are even more compelling. People with high Emotional Intelligence typically have less stress and anxiety. They report being happier, demonstrate better mental health and even experience improvements in their physical wellbeing. Increasing your self and social awareness also has huge payoffs in both the strength and satisfaction gained in relationships with your spouse, partner, friends, workmates, and relatives.

I wrote this book in an effort to help you think about and discover your own path to greater self and social awareness. Rather than following an academic approach with data and one-size-fits-all suggestions, I'm taking an indirect approach to your EI growth by pointing out some of the common sights you're likely to see while traveling on the open road. And I'm using them to explore your inward self and your outward relationships. I could have used freeway signs, bridges, rest stops, unusual vehicles, beautiful landscapes, or various types of architecture visible from the roadways, and yet I (oddly) decided to focus on highway debris.

I like the idea of using the insignificant stuff that falls out, flies out, or is intentionally thrown out of moving vehicles to consider the more significant inward, and regularly guesstimated areas of our human experience.

Think of this book as another form of "trash talk." Instead of directly (and insultingly) pointing to areas where you might need to up your game (and don't we all!), I'll use highway debris metaphorically. I'm confident that these pages will help you see yourself more clearly and provide solutions to unclutter your interactions with others. You will finish the journey with better insight and awareness about the people and situations that populate your life, and the person you are in those situations and among those people.

CHAPTER ONE

wanderlust

"One's destination is never a place, but a new way of seeing things."
– HENRY MILLER

He must have noticed my surprise despite my attempt to quickly conceal it because he immediately listed a string of reasons why he had never traveled more than 300 miles from his hometown. I was surprised. I knew that some people are not travelers by nature, but it still shocked me that this healthy and confident thirty-five-year-old man hadn't faced the need or acted on the desire to go... to travel and explore.

Since that conversation, I've met at least a dozen people in their thirties or forties who had never traveled outside of the state in which they were born. There are more people in that category than you would imagine. A study conducted by OnePoll[1] suggests this number could be as high as 11% of the US population. Most people say they would like to travel more, but when this 2019 survey asked how prepared they were to get away from home in cars, trains and planes, over 30% of participants indicated that they did not own or could not remember ever buying luggage.

Among those who do pack their bags and venture out, summer leisure travel is most common. I was surprised, however, to find that the average distance people cover from doorstep to destination is only 284 miles one way. Travel by trains and buses accounts for about 2% of leisure trips. Only 7% board planes for leisure travel, shoving their carry-on bags into large plastic overhead bins like a guy who really needs to be in a size–thirty-six pants but is trying to cram himself into a thirty-four. Flying, albeit fast, is the worst kind of travel in my opinion. You get to your destination (hopefully without as many delays and canceled flights as my last trip) but imagine all that you missed speeding along at 260 miles per hour at an elevation of 30,000 feet. The sights, unhurried pace, scenery, and the freedom to relieve my bladder without the captain turning off the "Fasten Your Seatbelt" sign are often all the motivation I need to bypass the TSA experience, load up the car, and hit the road.

Most leisure travel is undertaken by people who do just that. They load up their personal vehicles and get out on the highways in pursuit of recreation or to see family in various parts of the country. The long hours in traffic or hearing the dreaded "Are we there yet?" from impatiently confined children can make the most reasonable adults question their sanity for choosing to travel this way. Among the marginally sane recreational travelers, there are hundreds of thousands of professionals who earn their living by making their way along interstates, mountain passes, and back country roads.

These jobs place people behind windshields traveling over long stretches of gray pavement to make deliveries, conduct sales calls, build new things, repair broken things, or sing, dance, and act on stages. In one of his live-recorded concerts, James Taylor introduces a song by saying, "It's another traveling song. After a while, you get a lot of those."[2] In his fifty-plus years of performing and touring around the world, I'm sure James has more than a few traveling songs. Tolkien, in his book *The Fellowship of the Ring* introduces a few bits of rhyme sung by the hobbits known as "walking songs." They help the hobbits stay focused on the journey, giving some necessary courage to these, "creatures who prefer to stay in their cozy homes instead of venturing out into the unknown world beyond the shire."[3]

Traveling by car or RV strangely captivates me. Woven into the hazards and hassles of road trips, an internal thirst for exploration and a sense of wonder urges me on. I believe the same spirit that drove early explorers to forge rivers, ramble through canyons, and traverse mountain passes can be found to some degree in all of us. As much as our love of the comforts and security of home can work to suppress it, we each have an innate curiosity about the things that wait just around the next bend in the road or over the approaching crest of a hill.

A couple of centuries ago, people referred to this explorer's urge as *wanderlust*. I hope you never let fears or an exaggerated desire for comfort crowd out the desire to see, experience, and breathe in the air of places found miles and hours from your home.

Years ago, I worked with a man in his late forties. We were going over work schedules in preparation for a trip I was taking to Scotland when he commented that he'd heard how beautiful the countryside was in that part of the world. When I asked if he had ever traveled outside the United States, his reply caught me a bit off guard: "I'm more of an armchair traveler."

I had never heard armchair used in the context of traveling. He explained that instead of traveling, he regularly watched travel shows and documentaries. From the familiar environment of his small living room, he watched videos about destinations where his feet would never walk. He would never eat the food, see the local sights, or interact with the people who called that distant place "home." I walked away from that conversation a little sad for him.

I dreaded the way I had to travel to Great Britain: eleven hours on an airplane is not my idea of fun. But I will never forget the experience of climbing the steep, circular stairs of Scott Monument and the breathtaking view it offered over the city of Edinburgh or the smell of the sea air as I looked out over the English Channel from Aberdeen.

You might be happy to know that satisfying your wanderlust doesn't require traveling eleven hours by airplane to foreign countries. Walking through the canyons of skyscrapers in Manhattan, standing at the north rim of the Grand Canyon, driving through the green rolling hills of Kentucky, wading into the clear waters of Lake Tahoe, or letting your feet sink into the warm sand anywhere on the hundreds of miles of beach cradling the Gulf of Mexico are all reachable by bus, train, or automobile. You must only be willing to trade the comforts of staying put for the rewards of traveling to undiscovered places.

all around you on the road

Part of the intrigue of road trips is what you will see along the way to your destination. Your eyes drink in the landscape of snow-packed mountains, expansive farms and ranchlands stretching miles on end, jagged ocean shores, placid lakes, and rivers churning with whitewater over moss-covered boulders. Variations of architecture await you, including glass-flanked high-rises, cookie-cutter subdivisions, shopping malls, the beckoning lights of neon-draped casinos, ornate century-old stone buildings, white church steeples, and old barns that appear to be just one good windstorm away from total collapse.

You get to observe other vehicles sharing the road with you. Some brand-new sports cars bear personalized license plates, prompting you to try to make sense of the message by reading the letters and numbers out loud. Other vehicles appear to be beyond their better days with faded paint, dented fenders, and plastic taped over broken side windows.

You get glimpses of your fellow travelers in those vehicles. Some angry drivers aggressively tailgating car after car, letting the world know that they've got important things to do and everyone is in their way. Others wander lost in thought, miles away from the pavement they are driving on, oblivious to the buses, semitrucks, and cars motoring around them. My favorite is the solo driver you observe bouncing their head and singing their heart out as they enjoy a bit of private karaoke. I've been all those people.

Trips by car, bus, or RV also allow you to see clever creations placed out for display on the side of the road. I've driven by dozens of random, homemade sculptures of animals and dinosaurs, a few stuffed scarecrows sitting behind the steering wheels of rusted farm equipment, and hundreds of boxcars from transport trailers set out as cheap billboards, bearing hand-painted messages about politics, religion or encouraging travelers to take the next exit to find farm-fresh produce.

On a section of highway about forty miles from my hometown, someone fastened a mailbox atop a twenty-foot pole with "Air Mail" painted on the sides. Less than ten miles south of town, along a section of Interstate 5 skirted with cattle pastures, people have been decorating a dead tree with Christmas ornaments every year for as long as I can remember.

I find myself driving by these varied displays of creativity and randomness, trying to figure out what would compel people to make these quirky greetings and put them along the road. I haven't come up with any reliable answers to those questions. I am, however, glad they made the effort.

the debris you see

In addition to the novelties, fellow travelers, and scenery, road trips allow you to see items that fall out, fly out, or are thrown out of moving vehicles. Yes, you get to see the trash. In fact, I'm hoping you've noticed the staggering amounts of trash that accumulate on the center medians and sides of the road. Periodically you'll see large furniture items, full plastic auto bumpers, and home appliances abandoned on the gravel shoulders of the highway. Most of the roadside trash, however, is made up of construction debris, plastic containers, clothing, mangled tire treads, water bottles full of urine, bits and pieces of cars, aluminum cans, and food wrappers along with other paper debris. In 2019, the department of transportation removed 287,000 cubic yards of litter from freeways and interstate highways just in the state of California—enough to fill 18,000 garbage trucks![4]

I've traveled over much of the United States by car, and that windshield time has made me more alert to items that end up discarded on the side of the road. Through many years of travel, I'd found a way to see the beauty, creativity, and novelty of the landscape just beyond the polluted shoulders of the highway. Then, on a long, boring drive across the northern region of Nevada, I began seeing roadside trash differently. I started making notes on ways this roadside debris could relate to who we are as human beings and how we live and travel through our lives with others.

some metaphoric help

Hopefully, you've noticed the roadside trash for its environmental impact. As a society, we really need to pay more attention to the way we dispose of debris and stop polluting our public spaces. However, my primary purpose in pointing out this trash is to use it as metaphors and make larger observations about life, relationships, and self-awareness.

Metaphors offer imaginative ways to think about and understand ideas. You've likely heard life's troubles described as storms, a difficult educational process compared to climbing a mountain, or most interestingly, sex explained by talking about the birds and the bees. Metaphors allow you to take known or ordinary items and connect them to parts of life that are sometimes difficult to discern.

They also help us describe feelings or interpret internal experiences. I believe these debris metaphors can genuinely help you better understand who you are, your central being of thoughts, motivations, assumptions, values, and beliefs.

A metaphorical approach provides enough detachment from the observation to keep you from becoming defensive, yet it enhances mental connections between the kind of person you are as opposed to the person you hope to become. I aim to guide you in considering the valuable and lasting pieces of your life by looking at some of the discarded, broken, and worthless debris that ends up on the side of the road.

Some of you are asking, "So, you want to talk about roadside trash?" Yes, I do. Let's get out on the highway and take a drive!

CHAPTER TWO

broken pieces of automobiles

In high-traffic areas, plastic bumpers, taillight lenses, fragments of windshield and headlight glass, and twisted pieces of chrome commonly litter the roadways. This debris, along with paint-color scrapes on concrete median walls, point to evidence of collisions.

Automobile accidents happen all the time. I remember listening to a traffic reporter helicoptering over San Francisco-area highways. A particularly eventful commute day had resulted from the appearance of a nasty winter storm. Accident after accident snarled traffic for hours in all directions. The reporter signed off for the evening by saying, "OK, let's all go home, pound the dents out of our cars, and try this again tomorrow."

Smashed up bits of automobiles tell me there was an accident. I don't know the severity, the number of vehicles, or the degree of injuries. I just know that moving objects collided, and the fragments now pushed to the edge of the road bear silent testimony to the hazards of driving among thousands of other speeding objects.

people collisions

Outside their vehicles made of metal, plastic, and glass, people also collide. They run into situational obstacles and other people with life-changing force, and the debris of those collisions flies into the air. Though we experience people-to-people collisions at the very deepest levels of our being, we tend to quickly tidy them up and settle things outwardly so we can move on. To some degree, the ongoing momentum of jobs, parenting, and making rent and car payments relentlessly pushes us forward, urging us to clean up relational debris as fast as we can and get on with life.

A romantic relationship suddenly and painfully splinters; a final, angry decision fractures a marriage; or a long friendship ends with hostile words and bitter accusations. Yet there you are the next day, slipping on your work clothes, adjusting your necktie over a huge lump in your throat, or trying to apply enough makeup to disguise a sad and anguished face. Our rapidly moving lives do not seem to allow for the careful sorting through of broken debris, so we sweep it into cardboard boxes, seal them closed with some duct tape and toss them into the back corners of our souls.

We carry this unsorted brokenness in lives that appear to have undergone the quick repairs that body shops do with wrecked cars. A few new parts and some dent filler, and we merge back onto the highway, all polished up and smelling like fresh paint. Another collision will add new fragments to the mix, expanding the weights we carry, slowing us down, and making us cautious and untrusting.

learning about others

When you hurry through relationship collisions, sweep them up, and move on without pausing to learn what happened and why, you shortchange your social and emotional growth. Honest reflection after emotions have cooled offers you valuable insights about living with other humans and teaches you truths to carry forward in existing relationships. To a great degree your future happiness depends on this learning. Knowing how the people in your life respond to stress, anxiety, pressures, and unmet personal needs will equip you to act with empathy in some collisions and avoid other fender-benders altogether.

In my professional life, I've done a lot of conflict-resolution training for employees and managers in corporations. At their core, conflicts are mostly fueled by unmet needs. Individuals with low awareness of the needs of others end up having more conflicts. The most deeply entrenched conflicts happen when each party in the fight remains stubbornly focused only on what they need and resists any urge to empathize with the needs of their opponent.

During conflict workshops, I ask management teams to list the negatives and positives of conflict. The negative list is always longer by a dozen or more responses. I've had some groups struggle to come up with more than one positive benefit. At the end of the exercise, I make my best case for understanding the benefit of conflict resolution both to relationships and organizational culture. You can think about conflict as a revealing tool.

In organizations, conflict reveals system problems that are hard to detect on productivity reports. For individuals, conflict reveals unmet needs that are slowly wearing away the foundation of healthy relationship. Conflict strips away routine relationship behaviors that have allowed you to live isolated in your own head and mostly paying attention to what you want and need. Going (relationally) from fifty miles per hour to a dead stop with shattered glass and twisted metal around you, forces you to notice and consider what is present and true in the lives of others traveling on the same stretch of highway. Just like you, they have deep worries and fears. Just like you, they need inclusion, acceptance, belonging, and meaning.

A woman approached me after one of my training sessions, asking for advice on what to do in her relationship with her partner. She told me that they were in nonstop conflict and said, "I keep expecting him to change, and he never has."

I gave her the difficult-to-hear perspective that his lack of change may suggest that he is content to be as he is and is unwilling to invest the necessary energy to change. I said it could also be that she was only focused on what she expected him to change and had perhaps neglected to learn about him, his needs, and his long-developed responses when those needs were threatened or deprived.

"Well, I have needs, too. I need him to change!" she sputtered.

I assured her that I did not intend to invalidate what she said, but I wasn't sure the demand for him to change accurately described the needs that existed at the deeper level of her life. "What do you really need to feel valued, supported, happy, and content, to really thrive as a human being?" I asked. As she started listing them, I pressed a bit further, "How familiar do you think your partner is with your list of needs? What do you think would be on *his* list?"

It has taken most of my near forty years of marriage for me to understand how my wife responds when her personal needs go unmet. I can complain all day that her response is not helpful or effective, but that denies her individuality. She is who she is. Ignoring or misreading her responses as "she's in a bad mood" or "just being difficult" keeps me from seeing her true needs. That kind of assumption also results in missing early warning signs which precede screeching tires and colliding fenders.

Social intelligence (or social awareness) is the other half of Emotional Intelligence. Building skills to notice and name the emotional content in the lives of others is important to healthy relationships in general, but it is vital to your growth in learning from conflict. This is not random labeling. Drawing the conclusion that, "she's just narcissistic, or he's co-dependent and needs to grow up" does nothing to contribute to social awareness. In fact, labels like these only serve to cement our opinions into biases. Noticing and naming are humanizing efforts to see who the person is and discern what is driving their behavior. Identifying the presence of loneliness, confusion or grief provides helpful ways to respond to others, or at the very least contextualize their actions. Their emotional status and needs are likely being masked behind behaviors that are regularly getting reactions from people rather than empathy.

Most of us are peacekeepers. We don't look for opportunities to smash into others like wild-eyed kids driving bumper-cars at amusement parks. But when conflict happens, and it unavoidably will, it provides an extraordinary opportunity to learn what's behind a behavior, what's just part of human nature, and what's sitting at the critical center in the needs of others.

learning about yourself

As important as it is for you to learn about the needs and responses of others, you must also learn about yourself. Relationship collisions can provide the truest way of gaining this kind of personal insight. Self-discovery is much harder than it sounds. Nobel Prize laureate and behavioral economist Daniel Kahneman observes that human beings possess an "almost unlimited ability to ignore our ignorance."[5] His point is that we don't see ourselves accurately, hindered by obstructive layers of self-excusing and self-justifying rationale. In other words, we are magnificently proficient at fooling ourselves.

Self-insight involves an accurate and deep understanding of your own identity, motives, needs, abilities, and attributes. Imagine insight as the ability to *see in*. Accurately seeing into the central framework of your being may allow you to connect the effects of specific behaviors and relational dysfunctions to their subversive causes.

We often use the word "clueless" to describe people who don't understand how their actions or attitudes are creating the troubles they experience. Insecurities, disappointment at being overlooked or ignored, self-criticism, an unfulfilled need for recognition, shame, bitterness, or a wounded ego often show up in externalized behaviors like passive-aggression or disengagement that would be difficult for observers to connect back to their internal origins. Self-insight can reveal how the condition of your internal self is driving external decisions or behaviors. How well do you *see in* to your motives, values, and needs?

When you focus entirely on what the other person did to cause an accident, you ignore your contributions to relationship dysfunction. What frame of mind were you in before communication fell apart? What signs of trouble did you notice and dismiss? When relationship collisions happen, you can gain self-insight by considering your contribution to the accident.

Perhaps you've heard relationships referred to as bank accounts. If you haven't made enough relational deposits, a sudden withdrawal caused by a thoughtless action or disagreement can bankrupt a friendship. I used this example during a retreat for a regional credit union and had momentarily forgotten that all the attendees were banking managers. When I asked the question, "What happens when you withdraw more money than you've deposited?" everyone in the room pointed to one man and said, "You get to deal with Greg." Greg, it turns out, was the collections manager.

To grow in self-insight you'll need to ask yourself questions like, "Was I investing enough positive energy into the relationship to sustain it before we faced the collision of a misunderstanding, threat, or trouble? Asking honest, self-insight questions will help you grow in your Emotional Intelligence and better prepare you to resume highway speeds with others. You'll need to make a deliberate effort to maneuver around the large obstacles of the other person's accident-inspired resentful words and reactive behavior to a place where you can accurately see yourself. Owning your part of relationship malfunction is never easy to do. However, your future self (and everyone in that future) will be grateful that you made the effort.

building with broken pieces

My uncle Jim sent his mom two Chinese lanterns before he returned to the US at the end of the Vietnam War. They had been severely damaged in shipping, and the pieces had been shuffled from box to box and place to place before he finally showed them to me. At ten years old, I set out to fix them.

After days of gluing broken pieces of black plastic together and attempting to reapply painted silk panels that encircled the lights in two separate rings, I finally gave up. The debris was just too small, and too many fragments had gone missing to bring even one of the lanterns to wholeness.

Sometimes collision-broken people find commonality with and attraction to other collision-broken people and try to build something lasting and beneficial from the pieces. I'm not saying you should give up on others or yourself after life-shaping collisions. I am suggesting that you may want to sort through some of those sealed-up and tucked-away boxes from previous collisions with the help of a guide, therapist, or friend. Some fragments of past damage are simply unusable in the life you're attempting to build with others. Open up and talk about your moments of heartbreak or pain from these relational wrecks. Dump the unusable rubble in the landfill, and use the larger pieces to build a healthier, more insightful, and experienced you.

CHAPTER THREE

cargo straps

If I could ever locate my Boy Scouts' award patch for knot tying, I should probably return it to the officers of that organization. I would need to make a shamefaced surrender of the patch and offer a resigned admission that I can just barely tie my shoelaces, much less successfully secure a bowline knot, rolling hitch, or square knot.

I have a sneaking suspicion, however, that I'm not alone. The flat, woven nylon cargo straps you can buy in a four-pack at Home Depot for $12.99 have all but replaced the need for those nautical knots. These tie-down straps are ideal for those of us who have forgotten everything associated with tying knots, but they are not perfect. That evidence lies all along the roadways.

It's hard to miss the bright orange, yellow, green, red, or blue straps that lie strewn on the side of the road like deflated neon snakes. When I see them, I'm left to wonder what they were holding down. They were securing something, and now they are not. Suddenly I'm more alert to what dresser, ladder, or twin-sized pee-stained mattress might appear on the road just ahead.

These bright straps did have a purpose. They secured valuable things, holding down items that people didn't want to lose. The utilitarian straps themselves are not valuable but are designed to serve a practical purpose. We don't store them in velvet-lined boxes, take photos of them to show our friends, or attempt to keep them clean and attractive. They are simply designed to hold things down. I would suggest to you that there are also ordinary, utilitarian straps in your interior life that keep the weightier, more valuable things in place and fastened down, so they won't topple over from our lives' hard bumps and sudden sharp turns.

securing valuables

What holds valuable goals, people, and purposes in place for you? Are there practices or routines that keep the pieces of your life together? Traveling, staying in hotels, and eating out are enjoyable, but I find that they interrupt some of my typical routines.

At a business conference in Boston, I was chatting with an associate during a break between meetings. We complained about the miserable weather we'd had since arriving. She commented that she was about to lose it because she hadn't been able to get out and run for a few days. For a non-runner like me, that sounded like bliss. Throw a party: I don't have to get out and run today!

But for her, the routine of running was therapeutic. It provided quiet space in her day that allowed for internal sorting that she needed for clarity and sanity. With the travel and bad weather breaking up her routine, she was feeling out of sorts; things were in jeopardy of toppling over.

There is a great benefit to knowing which routines or habits keep the larger pieces of relationships, commitments, and values of your life in place. Are you keeping up with honest conversations, caring about the needs of others, unburdening your soul through meditation or prayer, regularly reminding yourself of the person you're aiming to be, and attending to your personal need for rest, quiet, exercise, and healthy eating? If you're not aware of what's gone missing in your routine, the loss of valuable anchors will catch you by surprise.

lost art of reflection

An important internal cargo strap for me is regular self-reflection. This EI practice helps me keep track of who I am, how I am, and what I've been doing among the people in my circle of relationships. My overstimulated, white-noise-filled world often hinders this kind of tracking, but I value how it helps me keep myself centered and self-aware. Distractions, however, are not the only hazard you'll face in attempting to practice honest self-reflection.

My good friend Mike says that when he takes on any new ventures, he imagines it like navigating a boat down a river. He says he always looks for the boulders downstream that could pose a problem as you move forward. Setting out with good intentions and optimism is fine, but knowing where you are likely to face pitfalls and resistance will prepare you to deal with them as they appear. The alternative is being caught off guard and unprepared at the sound of rock scraping metal and the appearance of water in the floor of the boat. Let's look at a couple of the potential barriers you could face in your efforts to honestly reflect on your actions and decisions.

the hazard of outside help

You may have tried to see yourself honestly by asking for input from a friend, family member, or a counselor. As much as you want people to be straight with you and tell you the truth, your self-protection instincts will regularly interfere with hearing that feedback. Truth from an outside source can cause you to become defensive, question the truth-teller's motives, or feel criticized.

Some people (even professionals) are better at giving constructive feedback than others, so you'll need to shop around and test the approach different people use and how that aligns with your expectations and needs. The most important thing you can do prior to inviting others to be honest with you, is to be honest with yourself about this boulder in the stream. Honest feedback will be difficult to hear. It is often painful and humbling. You will likely feel a strong need to defend yourself. Perhaps you'll even face the desire to turn the tables by looking for imperfections in the person providing the feedback. This is all normal. Prepare yourself to move around this hazard by getting clear about why this kind of feedback is important and reminding yourself that this experience will be difficult and will likely elicit defensiveness.

One other helpful suggestion is to learn how to "roll with the punches." We've normalized that phrase to mean, take life's hits and move on, but it's actually a training concept from boxing. To roll with a punch means to shift your body to align or agree with the direction of the punch so the force of impact is decreased (think of getting hit on the left side of your face and turning your head quickly to the right to absorb the impact). Rolling with the punches of honest feedback from others would mean agreeing with the direction of their observations and minimizing the pain of impact. You can do this by pushing past your defensive reactions and asking follow-up questions like, "Where else could you see this attitude limiting me?" or "What would you see as my first, best step to correct this behavior?"

the hazard of rumination and self-criticism

Some find honest self-reflection difficult because it quickly translates into feelings of worthlessness and self-criticism. You may end up ruminating instead of reflecting when you attempt to look backwards. Rumination fixates on negative experiences by replaying hurtful things others have done to you or the poor decisions and missed opportunities you've made yourself. Reflection uses remembering as a focused process allowing you to find ways to improve. The ability to honestly see how your patterns of thought, choices or behavior are either hurting or help-ing you covers most of the distance needed to navigate toward positive change. But if you tend to beat yourself up or get stuck replaying the memories of pain caused by things others have done to you, it can erase those gains in seconds.

Navigating around this boulder will require a discipline of your mind. Here are three actions that will help you avoid the hazard of rumination and self-criticism:

First, consider the timing. I know there are times when I am strongest and the most positive mentally, and I also know when I'm not at my best. What are yours? Reflecting on con-versations, decisions or events should not be done too far af-terward, but it's also not necessary to do this within a couple of hours. Identify the time when you are mentally strong and pos-itive and do your reflective searching for ways to improve then.

Second, consider the need for structuring. Having a set of questions that you answer as you look back can be extraordi-narily helpful in keeping you away from the boulders. I'll typ-ically use a set of questions in my self-reflection. "Who would I have needed to be to have ended up with a better outcome?" "What actions could I have done differently to have gained a better result? "What personal values did I reflect or deny by my actions?" "What attitude or frame of mind most influenced how I was and what I did?" "What did I learn about myself through this?" "What did I learn about the people involved in this?" "What is one specific piece of improvement advice I am taking away from this situation?"

Third, consider the need for confining. If you spend too long looking back, you'll open the opportunity for rumination. Negative situations hold their own emotional energy, so without boundaries they will play back through your mind like a video loop triggering repeated feelings of regret, anger, shame, or resentment. Your mind wants to work out a solution to the feelings, but there's no going backward.

The best way to stay focused on reflection for improvement and avoid rumination loops is to confine the time. Some of you have followed the pomodoro method where you create 25-minute intervals for working on specific tasks. Setting a simple timer is a great way to train your focus for achieving higher productivity, but this method can also be applied to confining the amount of time you spend in active reflection. As I said, this is a discipline of your mind, so don't hesitate to use controls like a timer to help your self-reflection yield the best possible results.

the hazard of wondering why

You may also have fallen into the *why* trap. This derails self-reflection by questioning why things are the way they are or why someone treated you the way they did. Those *why* questions feel insightful, but if you get stuck in only seeking something or someone responsible for the pain or difficulty you're experiencing, you could get sidetracked with blame and feelings of resentment. Both will keep you from finding truthful ways to see yourself.

Again, this is a boulder in the stream of self-reflection. It doesn't have to be a dam. The best ways I've found to move around the hazard of wondering why are: giving up on sense-making (more on that later) and strengthening your internal locus of control.

People fall into two general categories regarding their view of what happens in their life. Psychologists refer to these categories as an internal or external locus of control. If you believe that the source (locus) that determines what happens in your life is outside (external) of your control, you will be more inclined to blame other people or circumstances and take less personal responsibility. People who believe that the determination of what happens in their life is within their own control (having an internal locus) tend to be better off psychologically. The reason is simple; being a passive bystander to the events of your life contributes to feelings of helplessness, whereas taking action on what you can control offers hope and possibilities.

Here's a great way to get you started on strengthening your internal locus of control. Step one, write down what you want to achieve and list 8-10 steps that would be necessary to get there. Step two, highlight the steps which are within your control and leave the steps over which you have no control alone. Step three, create action plans that will use your strengths to move forward on the steps you highlighted.

avoid being blindsided

The kind of thinking I've been describing in the last few paragraphs is important for the development of your Emotional Intelligence. Emotions hold the most power to disrupt your best intentions in situations where you are blindsided by them. When you ride a rollercoaster at an amusement park you usually first have to wait in a long line (providing opportunities to carefully watch the faces of returning riders for signs of terror or trauma), then you step into the railcar, settle into your seat, and then you finally pull the restraining bar towards you until it locks in place. Moments later you are being rocketed down the track and jostled around without any control over what happens until the ride ends.

Getting hit with defensiveness, self-criticism, or resentment seemingly out of nowhere skips right to the click of the restraining bar and off you go... riding out the *feels* without much control over which way you are getting pushed and pulled. I said those hits come "seemingly" out of nowhere. The fact is your emotions are being triggered by situations, conversations and events that hold the predictive potential of producing them. Many of you already do this kind of preparation by giving yourself the "I won't let them get under my skin" pep-talk when you realize you're going to see the know-it-all uncle at Christmas, or you've been called into a meeting with a co-worker who oozes self-righteousness. The jump from being "fine" to "furious" or "doing okay" to "despondent" is shortest for people who live with low self-awareness. They are vulnerable to being caught off guard because of a failure to connect specific activities with the potential for experiencing related emotions.

The hazards I've listed for honest self-reflection are common emotional responses: defensiveness, self-criticism, and resentment. If you anticipate experiencing one of those, or perhaps other emotional responses based on your personality, you will be much better prepared to manage what you feel and skip the rollercoaster ride altogether. Anticipation won't stop the surfacing of certain emotions, but it can help you choose a different ride like the bumper cars... at least you have a gas pedal and steering wheel!

check the straps

When the tie-down of self-reflection finds its way to the gravel on the highway median, you will likely become much more aware of the actions, attitudes, and faults of others. The hard bump of an unexpected conflict can topple a friendship because you've lost sight of who you are or what you've done to leave the relationship unsecured and vulnerable.

Pamela recently asked me if I had heard from a friend who lives a few hundred miles away. My response, as I reflected on it later, was a somewhat negative characterization of him: "He's the kind of guy who, when you're on his radar, sends constant messages and touches base, but he then goes through periods when he gets busy with other things and disappears for months at a time."

Later, as I thought about my response, I realized he could just as easily say that same thing about me. Some internal reflection allowed me to own my lack of effort in connecting with him and work on tightening that strap.

strap tautness

In the summer of 2017, I had some consulting work to do in Ogden and Salt Lake City. My schedule allowed a few days between meetings, so I decided to take my motorcycle and spend those days riding through the magical landscape of southern Utah. I loaded my motorcycle onto a small trailer and secured it using six flat nylon straps and pulled out of my driveway to embark on the long, interstate trip.

After driving for a couple of hours, I stopped to grab a bite to eat. Before getting back in the car and continuing, I walked around the trailer and checked the tautness of each strap. It surprised me to find two of them were loose enough to be in risk of falling off and joining the other roadside debris, not to mention endangering the security of the motorcycle. I decided that I would do a walk-around check at every stop I made for fuel or food. I made only one stop on that 1,500-mile round trip when I did not need to adjust and tighten at least one of the cargo straps.

Movement on your journey will naturally shake, vibrate, and threaten to dislodge the important and valuable items you carry with you. Routines like self-reflection are hold-down straps that secure the items you want to keep in place when the hazards of the road introduce their toppling forces.

Check your straps!

CHAPTER FOUR

ice chest lids

Like colorful cargo straps, ice chest lids are hard to miss. . . rectangular white plastic contrasting with the gray concrete median or suspended in the branches of roadside foliage, they stand out like road signs letting other travelers know someone left something uncovered. The number of storage container and ice chest lids found along the highway seems to suggest that we put far too much confidence in small plastic fasteners. What power does the little snap on that Igloo cooler have against the seventy-mile-per-hour wind blowing across your open truck bed or the bow of your trailered boat? All you know is that it was there when you stopped for fuel in Omaha, and now that you've reached your campsite in Elkhorn, Nebraska, it's gone.

The lid is important for the function of the ice chest. It makes it handy for putting things in and getting things out, but the primary function of the lid is to maintain an environment in the chest that prevents things from spoiling. You may have only one use for ice chests, which is keeping your beer cold, but for a moment, let's just pretend that keeping food from spoiling might also be considered part of their useful purpose.

preserving relationships

I've discovered along my personal roadway that "keeping the lid on" certain activities contributes directly to the preservation of people and the relationships I have with them. A few years ago, a woman who had been volunteering at my non-profit came to see me at my office. She was seeing a spiritual advisor, and, taking this person's advice, she began meeting with various people and emptying her emotional well. What that meant in layman's terms was having a one-sided, purging chat with me about me and the organization I led. She politely asked me to not respond to anything she was about to say and proceeded to verbally vomit her criticisms, loathing, suspicions, and accusations on my desk. After she was finished venting, she smiled, thanked me, and walked out the door. She was obviously happy. I felt assaulted.

Knowing when to speak up or how to manage your feelings apart from explosively saying whatever is on your mind is another critical Emotional Intelligence skill. Perhaps you grew up in a home where it wasn't safe to express your opinions or have an open conversation in which you could get stuff off your chest. Repression of certain emotional and experiential content is not healthy. Finding your voice to speak what you think and how you feel is an important part of developing into a self-aware, balanced adult.

However, as with any good thing, too much is still too much. An ability to keep a lid on certain things we feel or think, can be vital to the preservation of another person's value, individuality, and most importantly their dignity. It alarms me how casually people use private information they know about someone to expose them and demean them in the eyes of others. I'm sure there is some psychological reason that compels one person to expose another person by telling their secrets, but sometimes we should stop examining reasons and just say it's wrong. We would do well to ensure that private information we know about others and most of the opinions, advice, and criticism we formulate about them stays securely under the ice chest lid when driving down the highway at seventy miles an hour.

Here are some ideas on ways to preserve your relationships.

keep the lid on things people tell you in confidence

To maintain good mental and emotional health, people need safe places to share the things they hold below the surface of their outward life. This includes burdens, troubles, fears, and ambitions. It also includes their secrets. The risk they take in opening those deeper areas of their souls to another person is subconsciously weighed against the costs of carrying those weights through life alone. Our collective community is healthier when its members have safe and trustworthy relationships to help unburden these weights.

When a person trusts you enough to disclose these secret things, it initially feels like a great honor, but that honor comes with some temptations.

People who are known as gossipers are using the secrets they know about others as currency to trade for status or approval to bolster their own insecurities. You have your own emotional needs and vulnerabilities, and in moments when you're feeling insignificant or unimportant, it can be tempting to disclose certain things you know about others to elevate your own status in a group.

You can also feel the pressure to share what you know about a person when you are participating in a *let's-fix-them* conversation with a mutual friend. Very little fixing happens when the subject of the conversation is absent, no matter how well-intended you are.

As you increase the in-the-moment awareness of your impulses and motivations, you'll be able to better manage any temptations to break a confidence that someone has entrusted to you. The bottom line is, unless a person is in danger of harming themselves or others, personal confidentiality is exactly that. People should be confident that you don't and won't share their secrets with others.

Keeping the lid on confidences preserves the dignity of others.

keep the lid on unsolicited advice

There is a fine line between telling someone about the benefits you are experiencing since going full-on vegetarian and making someone feel ashamed and stupid if they don't do as you have done. I've been told I should destroy my TV, exercise for two hours a day, read at least three books a month, cancel my Facebook account, write a personal letter to my children every week, and sell all my possessions and work on humanitarian projects around the world. This advice didn't all come from the same person or with the same emphasis. In some instances, people were just telling their story, and I felt the implied *should*. Others pushed so hard on their advising that it left me feeling I had no option other than to comply if I wanted to be good, right, healthy, or smart.

Wisdom informs us that advising others should be done cautiously and always in response to an invitation. Even when people ask for advice, it's best to frame suggestions in a broad-based way. For instance, "I'm not sure if this applies to every child, but this is what I've found works best to discipline my three-year-old." Human experience also shows that there is a point of readiness people need to reach which then allows them to hear and receive helpful advice. My estimation of a person's readiness for guidance is consistently misaligned with theirs.

Refusing to share overly opinionated and unsolicited advice provides the opportunity for people to seek out that kind of guidance when they see the need for it and are ready to hear it.

Keeping the lid on unsolicited advice preserves space for people to find what works for them.

keep the lid on criticism

There's a reason no one likes to be criticized: It doesn't help! I'm typically aware of the things I'm doing that just aren't working.

Mostly, I keep doing them because I don't know what else to do. All critics do, if you think about it, is state the obvious without any effort or energy to help. Who welcomes that? That may be all critics do, but that's far from all that criticism does. Advice, (even the uninvited kind) at least carries the intention of help through offering a suggestion. Criticism, on the other hand, expresses disapproval by pointing out mistakes as a matter of conclusion, "You're a screw up and you're screwing everything up."

As a result of people being people, you will have regular opportunities to observe humans making poor decisions and appearing to be ignoring the problems created by them. If they persist in behaviors that are making things worse, your thought pattern might move from "*Surely* they know how stupid that is..." to, "Apparently they *don't* know how stupid that is..." and ultimately to, "I need to *tell* them how stupid that is..." You can feel you are helping them by bringing what they are doing wrong to their attention. They obviously need an intervention... a tough love conversation. But for some strange cosmic reason, criticism never seems to produce the intended outcome.

Often the best help is to keep the criticism to yourself. The pavement of life is hard, and it hurts like hell when you hit it, but it is an effective teacher. Your words of criticism can work against life's teachings because you give people someone to blame and focus on instead of themselves.

Some families, having carried years of concern for a person battling a substance addiction, will wisely hire a professional to conduct an intervention. This keeps stressed-out family members from spilling emotion-fueled shaming lists on the person suffering the addiction (which are impossible to un-say), and it keeps the addicted person from creating blaming lists based on the personalities and history they have with the family. Keeping your criticisms under the lid removes you from the blame-lane leaving the people you care about on an unobstructed path to deal with the consequences of their own choices.

The other downfall of criticism is the way it boxes people in. When mistakes are pointed out as statements of conclusion, "You have made a complete mess out of this..." it's like closing the doors and windows on a room. There's no light of hope or opportunity for improvement. Critical language is concise. Interventionists feel no need to beat around the bush. This is what it is. But critical language is also dark and hopeless. Be ready to be helpful when people hit the pavement and become open to choosing a different path, but until then you'll help them more by keeping your judgments about what they are doing to yourself.

Keeping the lid on criticism preserves hope.

keep the lid on excessive venting

The insights and suggestions I've offered up to this point have been about preserving others by keeping the lid on things you know or would want to say about them. My observations in this last section have to do with limiting what you say out loud concerning your own life.

Life is not easy. It seldom seems fair, and we regularly encounter people and conditions that make difficult situations astonishingly more difficult to endure. It's my belief that as we have moved away from having deep conversations with trusted, long-term friends or observing spiritual practices like prayer and confession, we neglect regular emotional catharsis. As I mentioned a few paragraphs ago, human beings need private places to process the inward burdens, struggles, and disappointments they carry, but many of those places in our current culture have not been cultivated or accessed.

Social media is a profoundly poor replacement (owing to shallow comments that seek to fix you with a sentence or perhaps the even more unhelpful response of a thumbs up or heart emoji), but that doesn't seem to keep people from using these platforms for airing their struggles or complaints. After receiving some advice to seek out a counselor and a few recommendations to refrain from posting her frustrations about others on her Facebook feed, a young lady I know responded with, "This is my way of venting, so I don't really care about nor am I asking for your comments or opinions."

Continually venting your frustration can convey to everyone that there's only one way to make you happy: let things always go your way. The egocentric in you may say, "Good, glad we got that settled!" However, as a human being in relationship with other human beings, you need to remain aware of the impact produced by this narrow definition of happiness. Your continual venting makes it appear that you can be hard to please.

You, like this Facebook user, may not realize how venting impacts the way others perceive you and how it can alienate relationships. Not many people desire to spend time in that kind of negativity. Friendships require mutual benefit and shared enjoyments. If you want people to enjoy your company and be themselves around you, you must find a regular, private cathartic process that allows you to at least regulate what you vent about, and how often you do it.

That's the outward-facing side of say-whatever-you-feel-and-think expressions, but there are also personal implications associated with excessive venting. I believe that the anti-suppression folks have overemphasized the psychological benefits of expressing everything you think and feel. There are benefits to free and open expression to be sure, but there are also a couple significant personal drawbacks beyond those that impact your relationships.

One of these drawbacks is that venting can replace thinking. Some of the difficulties you face in life are rooted in unchangeable situations and the comfort of expressing the frustrations and being heard helps you to endure these difficulties. Many of the difficulties you face, however, require a solution. Venting your frustrations provides no real help in problem solving because that process involves solid thinking practices like defining and analyzing, along with solution-seeking practices like creative thinking and brainstorming. Venting only describes the injustice of situations as they are, and that can crowd out your ability to think through possible solutions to how things might be.

Another personal drawback to excessive venting is what I call the "talking placebo." Before I started coaching, I helped people by listening to them and offering some tools or practical advice. It took a while, but I started noticing how the process of talking about actions they wanted or needed to do gave my clients a sense of accomplishment that satisfied, and would often replace, the act of doing. One man had an extended and detailed description of what he wanted to say to his father to clear the air and get things out in the open. Every time we met, he would process his frustrations and tell me exactly what he wanted to say, yet he never did it.

Researchers have concluded that telling people what you want to achieve creates a premature sense of completeness. Just talking about your intentions provides an artificial emotion similar to the way you might feel after having actually completed them. The talking and venting for this guy was acting as a placebo, bringing a sense of satisfaction that mimicked a feeling of accomplishment. You do need to have opportunities to voice things you think and feel, but you'll help your overall mental and emotional wellness by regulating times for frustrated venting with opportunities for active problem-solving.

Keeping a lid on excessive venting helps preserve joy in relationships and contributes to a better thinking and action-oriented you.

securing the lid

You must actively work to preserve relationships. The thoughtless assumption that I can just be me, doing and saying what seems right and works for me, is like trusting the plastic snap lock that supposedly holds down the lid on the ice chest. Relationship spoilage can be prevented. Just make sure to keep yourself and others adequately covered.

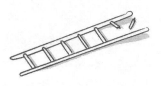

CHAPTER FIVE

ladders

Due to their size and shape, ladders are typically carried on the outside of vehicles. You'll often see them stuck in the beds of pickups like tall men lying awkwardly on very short mattresses, they extend beyond tailgates, their rigid legs and rubber feet angling slightly upward toward the sky. At other times you'll see ladders lashed to the racks of trucks, or perhaps you'll notice them hanging on the sides of panel vans, ready to be pulled off and put to work.

In my travels I've noticed that a surprising number of ladders end up bent and mangled on the side of the road. Unlike cardboard, paper trash, and plastic lids from containers or ice chests, ladders pose significant traffic hazards because they tend to stay where they land. I've been in a few traffic jams caused by ladders that had dislodged from vehicles and lay on the asphalt like silent protesters, blocking a lane or two of traffic.

Having used ladders in a construction job I held while in my last year of high school and first year of college, and again during the time that I owned a window coverings business, I feel an extra bit of sadness for the people who have lost them among the roadside debris. It's difficult to lose a tool when you are a tradesperson. Good tools aren't cheap and every minute you're at Lowes or Home Depot replacing them, you're falling further behind on your jobs. Losing a ladder presents a unique sort of loss because, while you may be able to ingeniously find a work-a-round for a missing tool by the creative use of a different one, there's just no way to MacGyver your way up a twenty-foot wall.

In terms of function, a ladder has only one: it helps people climb upward. I've found that people and opportunities function like ladders in our lives, providing ways for us to advance or move up personally and professionally.

upward movement

Our humanity draws us to be upward movers. Jerry Seinfeld makes a brilliant observation in one of his stand-up routines.

He compares how instructions from an adult to a child have a downward orientation: "Just calm down, slow down, come down here, sit down, put that down, keep it down in there," while everything in the aspiration of a child is upward: "Wait up, hold up, shut up, I'll clean up, let me stay up!"[6]

Through the years, I've met a few people who didn't seem at all interested in upward movement. They were the exception to the norm, and even in this exception, I was not convinced that upward movement was completely off their radar. I think it was more that their ladders were leaning against artistic, self-actualizing, or spiritual walls as opposed to the corporate or achievement kind.

From time to time, ladders (people and opportunities) that have helped us move up in the past may become dislodged from our lives and end up lost somewhere on the side of the road. The company owner who believed in you and kept inviting you into new roles sells the business, or a manager who had provided similar opportunities transfers to another part of the country. Your ability to roughly calculate margins in your head and win over clients with near-enough proposals is suddenly eclipsed by a twenty-seven-year-old with a tablet in her hand, tapping out exacting ROI over multiple years in less than a minute.

You hit a jarring shift in the pavement, and without warning that relationship, role, or skill that had always helped you move up is gone. It happened to me at twenty-nine. I realized that I had personally and professionally stalled out after eight years at the same job, so I resigned and enrolled back at the college I had left a few years earlier and got to work on finishing my degree. I also decided to volunteer some time in a non-profit business to keep developing my practical skills while college professors were packing my head with theoretical knowledge.

Soon after volunteering I had a lunch meeting with the CEO of the non-profit. About halfway through the meal he looked at me and said, "You do know why you're here don't you Jack?" I answered that I was there to help and learn (which I thought was a fair and direct response). Without hesitation, he said, "You're here to get retooled. You're like an old factory that has been producing widgets for years, but there's no longer any need for those widgets, so you're here to have some new equipment installed, and that will allow you to start producing something that people want and need."

I thought twenty-nine was a little young to be called an "old factory" and I felt justified in the right to be offended by what he said. But I knew (at least in principle) that he was right. I had gone as far as I could with what I had. I hadn't had many positive mentors walking with me and now the ladder of my abilities and skills was lost and broken on the side of the road.

missing ladders

You will have, as I did, a strong impulse to replace the tool of upward movement as quickly as possible. Ambition always finds a way to move forward, but what if the loss is revealing something important to your growth as a human being? The rebound factor we often talk about in romantic relationships has a similar type of expression in careers and even friendships. Unhealthy dependencies on people, and identities that are inappropriately tied to your job or what you do are especially difficult to recognize until those roles and relationships change or end. I thought I was doing just fine and only needed a quick tune up and a new opportunity. What I actually needed was an overhaul.

Emotional Intelligence isn't only about feelings. High or low EI also determines how open, flexible, and adaptable you are to new ideas and experiences. People who dig in and rigidly resist change become obstacles around which everyone else must navigate. Most don't see their own resistance because they're too busy scrambling to keep the pieces of their life in place that provide normalcy and predictability. If changes in your skills, roles or helpful relationships sends you searching desperately for the quickest possible replacement you would do well to focus on developing greater adaptability... and by the way, Home Depot doesn't sell it!

Acceptance is the kingpin to adaptability. Accepting the change that unavoidably follows the disappearance of people, role or skill ladders will help you pivot and make progress. The primary truth I had to accept when my role changed and it became apparent that my skills were no longer effective, was that there were ways of thinking and doing that were better than what I possessed. Had I resisted that acceptance, I would have sought another opportunity to do more of what I had already done only to face another crisis of upward movement a few months down the road.

The most important suggestion I can offer is to pause and take some time to psychologically adapt to the way your life has changed without that reliable ladder strapped to your vehicle *before* you go out hunting for a new upward moving relationship or opportunity. One of our self-inflicted wounds as humans is to not patiently remain in the process of transformation until its full work is complete.

Adaptations to new realities when relationships change or redefining your identity apart from the job you do or skills you possess is a transformative process. I relate it to taking antibiotics. You feel miserable so you see the doctor who tells you that you've got a sinus infection and prescribes antibiotics. The prescription instructions are to take one pill a day for ten days. By day four, you're feeling better and by day six your improvement makes you question the need to take the rest of the medicine, so you throw the bottle with the remaining 4 pills into the back of your medicine cabinet and resume the normal activities of your life. Two weeks later you're sick again. You felt better, but the infection wasn't gone.

I believe that our panicked drive to get back to normal produces incomplete healing, stunted personal growth, and poor understandings of our own soul. How can we experience the kind of deep and meaningful change we want and need when we always try to shortcut the slow adaptive process that genuine change requires? No matter who promises a better pill or program, the truth is that change takes place most effectively and enduringly when it occurs slowly. You'll grow significantly in your Emotional Intelligence by making a positive adaptation to unexpected changes. Then take the time to figure out how to balance life again on your own before attempting to add another thing to pursue or a person to occupy the empty seat on your sofa.

paying it forward

Another healthy way to look at a ladder ending up among highway debris is to consider whether it's time to do for others what has been done for you. My self-focus steers me immediately back into the lane of trying to find who will help me in my ambitions and pursuits. Could it be that this shift indicates a time for some pay-it-forward activity on my part?

Our culture uses the expression that we are "standing on the shoulders" of people who have worked hard and paved the way for those who are shaping the world today. With all the encouragement we give people to continue grinding, driving, and achieving despite their age (think of age-driven expressions such as "fifty is the new forty"), when, exactly, do we stop standing on the shoulders of others and allow others to stand on ours?

You don't have to make this "helped" to "helping" transition in your career if this is not the right time, but in terms of your growth in Emotional Intelligence, it would be worth some thought to consider this kind of shift in your friendships and perhaps even in your romantic relationships. Acting as a ladder of upward movement for others instead of desperately trying to find a new one to climb yourself will help your relationships immensely, and it is good for your soul.

CHAPTER SIX

black rubber

Most of the tire failures I've experienced have been the slow, seeping kind in which you start noticing an unusual side-to-side movement in the car while you're driving. This is the kind of tire failure you walk out to in the morning when you're already running late for work. You discover a flat, deflated tire, and your mood quickly follows.

I'm thankful that I've had only two tire blowouts in my driving years: once in a car and another time when I was pulling a camp trailer in the desert region of southern California just before crossing into Arizona. The trailer incident was the most alarming, shredding the trailer tire into a ring of mangled rubber.

The torn chunks and strips of black rubber that end up on the side of the road result from this kind of sudden blowout. Semi-trucks seem to be the largest contributors to this kind of highway trash. The speed, high pressure, and heavy burdens on truck tires combine to make their failures spectacular and messy. Several times during my travels, I've had to swerve quickly to avoid hitting flying chunks of tire rubber exploding suddenly from beneath a box trailer on the road just ahead. The National Highway Transportation Safety Administration reports that tire blowouts alone cause nearly 23,000 auto accidents each year. Most of these incidents happen in the summer months when hot temperatures, fast speeds, and overloaded vehicles set up conditions for unusually high rates of tire failure.

people blowouts

It's tempting to view blowouts between people as confrontations over the way you are being treated or disagreement over morality, politics, or behaviors. But I'd like to suggest that many of our relational blowouts result from the same factors involved with tire failures: speed, high pressure, and heavy burdens. We regularly lose track of growing internal pressures and their weight that has accumulated in our souls while we're speeding along from one event to another, meeting deadlines and managing calendars.

A few months ago, I watched an altercation between a pedestrian and the driver of a car in my hometown. The driver pulled up to a stop light, ready to make a right turn, just as the pedestrian stepped into the crosswalk. I'm trying to find the right word to describe the pace at which the pedestrian moved through the crosswalk. I want to call it a saunter, but perhaps it was more of a mosey.

Whatever it was, it was far too slow for the patience of the man waiting to make his right-hand turn. I watched in disbelief as the driver proceeded to roll down his window and shout something at the pedestrian, who then stopped completely in the crosswalk, blocked the car, and shouted back. The windows on my car were up, so I was left to interpret what might have been exchanged through the red faces, raised arms, and frequent protrusion of middle fingers.

What caught my attention was how quickly this hostility erupted between two complete strangers on an ordinary Tuesday morning. The blowout was between two men headed in different directions at different rates of speed, but there was likely much more involved than what transpired between them on the corner of South and Court streets. It seemed odd that they were both so poised for a fight. It was as if they had been bitter rivals since high school, and this intersection had caused their paths to cross, triggering an eruption of hatred that had been brewing for twenty long years. But this blowout was more than likely fueled by each man's internal weights and pressures. and had nothing whatsoever to do with each other. Indeed, most of your blowouts with people are not exclusively about them, nor are their blowouts exclusively about you.

self-insight and self-awareness

The key to understanding these internal weights and pressures is found in gaining better self-insight and self-awareness. I've used both terms in explaining Emotional Intelligence throughout these pages. Perhaps it would be good to differentiate between them.

Self-insight explains how your current choices or behavior links back to your motives, needs, or the way you perceive yourself and your abilities. After fifteen years in a career that required intense levels of interaction with large numbers of people, I finally realized how I had been suppressing my introversion to manage role-related activities better suited for an extrovert. This insight didn't lead me to change careers, but it did help me to make modifications to my peopling versus non-peopling schedule. These adaptations allowed my introverted self to breathe more freely.

Self-awareness is the ability to see in real time the thoughts and feelings you are experiencing as they are happening. This in-the-moment ability allows you to adjust by making insight-informed choices rather than merely reflecting on what happened after a sudden catastrophic blowout. The insight I gained about my introverted needs made sense of certain patterns of behavior and the way I have held relationships. It was like finding a puzzle piece that explained much of my history. Noticing and making current, proactive adjustments when I'm feeling people-fatigued or responding to the pressure of invitations to social gatherings is a function of self-awareness. Self-awareness is primarily about noticing.

the act of noticing

Noticing is important to our movement through life. We spend large parts of our days merely checking items off our to-do lists or reacting to people, events, and expectations. This nonstop movement produces a dust trail that leaves evidence that something happened but obscures the details of that activity. Many times my wife, Pamela, asks me how my day went and what happened, and I have to make a genuine effort to recollect and pull fragments of conversations and events out of the dust.

Somewhere in the blur of hurried activity, you are getting signals (mostly internal) that what is happening in that moment needs or deserves a second look. That second look can help you to see where internal pressures are building. It can make you aware of a personal vulnerability someone is exploiting to manipulate you. Or help you see how you're using a particular behavior to avoid a place of pain.

I often wonder how much clarity, self-understanding, and wisdom I'm missing because I'm bypassing the signals and second-look vista points as I speed along to my destination. These critical moments of self-awareness can point to the source of internal pressures that are building toward a blowout.

decompression

The chunks of black rubber on my personal highway are reminders of the need for some regular decompressing and soul care. Stress, uneasy relationships with family, and concerns about money, health, and aging parents (along with many other weights) contribute directly to the occurrence of blowouts. I can't carry that much at my rate of speed without risking sudden high-pressure failures that send fragments of black rubber flying across the highway.

Human beings face the need to forgive others (often), keep short accounts, and make sure the things that need to be said, get said. We need to give some people grace for their behaviors and carefully clarify our expectations of others. We need to regularly have meaningful conversations about our cares and fears with someone we trust. It's not as important to seek a fix for those things as it is to talk about them out loud.

Failing to regularly decompress and adjust your inward weights sets you up for blowouts. Take care of yourself. Act on the things that will not change without some attention and effort, and learn to let go of the things that are outside your direct control. You will be emotionally healthier if you do.

CHAPTER SEVEN

broken furniture

I was driving north on State Highway 99 in California near Manteca when I suddenly had to veer around the splintered wood carcass of what was once a dresser. At least I *think* it was a dresser. Come to think of it, I'm not even sure the city I had just passed was Manteca.

No, I had not been drinking and driving. The confusion over the demolished piece of furniture reflects the degree of demolition. The confusion over the name of the city results from city-namers (whoever they are) getting stuck somewhere in the middle of the English alphabet as they got to the middle of the Golden State. I've been amazed and confused for years by the number of cities linked by this highway that all begin with the letter M. From south to north, across an eighty-nine–mile stretch of highway, you pass Madera, Merced, Modesto, and Manteca. Anyway, I think it was a smashed-up dresser on the highway, and I know it was near a city on Highway 99 that begins with M.

What caught my attention besides the hazard in front of me was the volume of debris. I've seen other furniture remnants on the side of the road, including a recliner, a coffee table, bookshelves, and multiple white-plastic patio chairs with one or two broken legs lying awkwardly on the ground. But the impact when that dresser irrecoverably leaned out of that truck or trailer and crashed down onto the pavement must have been spectacular.

The dresser also caught my eye because I could see it wasn't like a lot of other broken furniture constructed from manufactured pressed board. That material tends to break apart like graham crackers, snapping into flat, fake-woodgrain chunks. This solid-wood piece of furniture broke up differently when it hit the pavement. *Shattered* is the best word, and I found myself wondering what that wood-meets-pavement spectacle looked and sounded like when it happened.

Continuing my trek, I wondered if the driver of the vehicle witnessed the misfortune. Were they distracted by their Doritos, Pepsi, and loud country music, only to realize the dresser's fate when they showed up at their destination? Were they clueless about the mishap, having no idea where, how, or when it went missing?

Another theory bouncing through my head was that perhaps the driver of the vehicle saw the splintering crash in their rearview mirror and chose to just keep driving. No point in returning to the place of destruction. It would be unsalvageable, a total loss.

functional and sentimental

Furniture can play dual roles in our lives. First, it serves a function. It holds our socks, helps us organize our DVD movie collection, or provides a place to sit and rest. We feel the loss of the item in respect to the fact that it no longer serves the purpose it once did. A cardboard box is not a suitable replacement for a morning coffee resting place. Losing a coffee table off the tailgate of a pickup sets up the need to get an item of similar function.

Furniture also plays a sentimental role. A bookshelf may have been of the cheap, pressed-board variety, but the fact that it was a hand-me-down from a friend or relative makes the experience of losing it feel somewhat different.

My socks, T-shirts, and other folded articles of clothing are stored in a solid-oak, six-drawer, upright dresser that once belonged to Pamela's grandparents. Over 100 years old, the drawers stick on their wood tracks if you don't pull them out evenly. It's missing the look and convenience of new dressers—no smooth-glide, self-closing hardware on this cabinet.

But the value does not derive purely from the piece's appearance or functionality. It has history. It has been connected to people who mean something to my wife and I, and that meaning has become attached to the piece of furniture they once owned. The loss of sentimental items is compounded by the fact that while the functionality of the item can be replaced, its history and connection cannot.

grieving loss

Loss triggers grief, and grief is a mysterious thing. I only associated it with the death of people until I read *Depression: Coping and Caring* by Dr. Archibald Hart. He redefined it as the psychological response to the loss of anything. Most people don't know what to do with the weird sadness that follows the loss of a job, moving from one city to another, or the ending of a friendship. We minimize these types of losses because they can't compare with the greater loss of death, but somehow our psyche still registers a loss, and that loss produces grief.

Over the course of several years, I met regularly for coffee with a man named Larry. He was in his late seventies when we began these every-other-week meandering conversations. Larry had been a pilot during World War II. After being drafted as a teenager and quickly completing flight school, he found himself flying supply planes over the Himalayan mountains between India and China (a path known as "the hump"). As our conversations went on and he wove old memories into newer ones, he talked about his experience with aging. When Larry would reflect on the later stages of his life, he described what I recognized as grief when he was forced to accept that he just couldn't do certain activities any longer.

Most of these activities were recreational, such as hiking and snow skiing, but he also wrestled with having to hire someone to do some things around the house that he had always done himself. Larry was not a run-to-a-therapist kind of guy, but I could tell by the comfort and ease with which he talked about these things, that talking about them had been his way of processing the sadness of loss. It was like standing with him at one of those scales that used to hang in the produce sections of grocery stores. Each loss was named and weighed, though not in some pity party or sympathy-seeking way. It was an honest consideration of what he had lost and what that loss meant to him. Some things weighed much more than others.

How do you grieve? Are you driving so quickly and so focused on where you're going that you don't notice what you've lost along the way? Perhaps you are like the people who may have watched their antique dresser fall to its demise along the highway behind them and just kept on driving. Someone would interject "No use crying over spilled milk." I agree, so long as we are only talking about milk. But friendships, relationships, roles, and neighborhoods are not replaced in half-gallon plastic containers found at the corner market or drawn freshly from Bessy-the-cow's renewable supply.

It is important to return (if you can) to the scene of the loss. Collecting the debris of what fell out and broke enables you to weigh the loss of a person, role, or relationship and to consider what purpose, function, and meaning the person or thing had in your life.

resisting the positive spin

American culture seems driven by the need to spin everything in a positive direction immediately. "Don't worry, you'll find someone else." "He didn't deserve you anyway." "You never really seemed happy in that job. It was probably just a stepping-stone to your dream job, which you never would have found had you not been let go from this crappy one."

We don't realize how this make-you-feel-good-quick hindsight assessment truncates the normal and healthy process of loss and grief. The encouragement to maintain positivity and to not look back has contributed to multitudes of people moving forward without reflecting on mistakes made at work and in relationships that directly contributed to their dissolution. In the loss of a friendship, relationship, or a job, sitting in sober and honest consideration of what happened cultivates healthy Emotional Intelligence.

Even our approach to funerals has fallen prey to the positivity quest. In lieu of memorials, many people are choosing to have "celebrations of life." I get that people want to honor the departed person, but this approach avoids the vital process of standing in the wreckage of loss. Feeling it. Suffering with it. In processing grief, we reconfigure the new normal of our life apart from the presence of the person and the functional place the relationship held for us.

You may be wondering why I turned on the sad faucet and what you need to do to turn it off. I hear that, but this truth needs to be said. Our humanity requires that we honestly and authentically grieve loss. Things are falling out of our vehicles and breaking on the road. Some of the damage is recoverable; some is not.

A few years ago, Pamela and I attended a Celtic music concert. The music was beautiful but dominated by haunting, tragic tales. At one point, one of the band members introduced a song by telling the story of how, during a break from the tour, he had written the saddest song he had ever composed. He was so excited to share it with the group when they got back together in the studio. But after hearing another group member's song, he disappointedly admitted that he had written "a sadder song than mine." I had no idea that sad music had a scale or that this was a desirable goal.

As I thought about it, the core of this musical genre honestly recounts real-life events. Strip away the glib, positive-spin responses, and you are forced to find language that lets you weigh and reflect on what was that is no more. We need that language. We must have the kind of weighing and sorting conversations like I had with my friend Larry. I encourage you to be mindful of the things that you have lost somewhere on the highway. Go back and consider whether a loss is recoverable or whether you need to genuinely grieve before jumping back into the driver's seat, mashing down on the gas pedal, and moving on.

CHAPTER EIGHT

hats

I recently realized that in all my careful noticing of highway debris, I've never seen a cowboy hat. You'd think this style of hat would be more susceptible to blowing out of an open window with its lightweight construction and wide brim. It could be that cowboy-hat wearing is less common in my part of the country. It could also be that a cowboy-hat wearer's attachment to their head adornment causes them to do whatever is necessary to retrieve it.

Most of the hats I see among the roadside debris are baseball caps. I've seen old worn caps that might have blown out of trash containers on the way to a landfill, and I've seen brand new caps, the kind that tempt me to pull over to the side of the road and play a little finders-keepers.

Once I was driving through the San Francisco Bay Area, and just after hearing a sports report on the radio about a horrible loss suffered by the 49ers, I spotted a Niners' ball cap nested with road debris against the center median on Interstate 80. I imagined a frustrated fan ripping the cap off his head and chucking it out the window of his car, uttering a string of expletives. I'm sure that's possible, but it's more likely that good ball caps end up on the side of the road courtesy of people in convertibles or those who lean too far out of an open window while speeding down the highway.

For most people, what we wear is a part of our identity. When people find a piece of clothing that makes them feel more attractive, comfortable, or confident, they tend to keep and use those items until they are too worn to wear anymore. As I was shopping for a couple of dress shirts at a men's clothing store a few years ago, a salesman walked up with a dark-blue tweed sportscoat and asked me to try it on. The moment I looked up and saw myself wearing it, I felt good. Good is a bit of a clumsy word to use because there were a lot of different feelings and impressions that I experienced in that single moment. I just knew I liked how I looked and felt wearing it. It's still in my closet after all these years and remains one of my favorites. Hats are significant in apparel identity. For some, whether they're endorsing a team or brand, or it's just a fixture of their look, their hat is a part of who they are. For example, think of actor and director Ron Howard.

A guy I know caught me completely off guard when I saw him for the first time without the black newsboy cap that had always covered his nearly bald dome. He looked completely different without the hat. It was a bit shocking. That hat, for my friend, had become a significant part of the way I knew and recognized him. I began to wonder whether something I wear identifies me to others.

What image do I project, not just in clothing but in the social behaviors I adopt, when I'm around people I don't know very well? Being the center of attention, playing the tough guy, always filling dead space in conversations with opinions or self-promotion, overtalking, playing the wallflower, being funny, or staying busy by helping, can all function to establish one's identity in a new group or to overcome social anxiety.

social coping behaviors

Can you identify the social behaviors that are a significant part of how people would identify you? What is it that makes you feel more comfortable in social settings? Is there something you rely on when trying to impress or gain the approval of another person? We rarely recognize how our overuse of certain social behaviors works against meaningfully connecting with others. Think of these as social coping behaviors. When you attempt to make yourself more comfortable through the overuse of a social coping behavior, it can make other people feel less comfortable. These coping behaviors can also become part of your social identity, shaping the way that others relate to and respond to you.

At a dinner party my wife and I attended along with five other couples, a woman at our table dominated the conversation. Literally, she never stopped talking. No one doubted her intelligence. In fact, we were often surprised by how much she genuinely knew about every subject that surfaced. However, her social coping behavior of dominating the conversation became a liability.

Learning how to be yourself and not overuse certain social behaviors forms the foundation of socialization. Interacting with other people can make one anxious and uncomfortable. I'm an introvert, so I get it. Discomfort will cause most of us to resort to a default social coping behavior. Overtalking is a common one. The lady at the dinner party ignored the cues other people were giving that her overtalking was turning them off.

At the other extreme, some people use shutting down or "wall-flowering" as a social coping behavior. They assuage their discomfort in social settings by disengaging. They avoid conversations, making steady eye contact with others, and may only respond to questions asked of them with "Yes," "No," or "I don't know." They disengage to cope with their discomfort in social settings and pray others won't try to get them to reengage. It's important to notice that the overuse of social coping behaviors may make you comfortable, but they can prevent social connections by disregarding the social needs of others.

It's likely that the hat of your social coping behavior is connected to who you are in terms of your introversion, extroversion, or other complexities of your past experience and personality. Don't feel the need to get rid of it entirely. Just recognize when your anxiety pushes that behavior into overuse and adjust to move incrementally in the opposite direction. Pushing into your personal discomfort zone allows you to remove that identity hat for a while.

negative social coping behaviors

Criticism, sarcasm, and one-upping fall into the category of negative social coping behaviors. These behaviors are not just harmful to healthy social interaction. They contribute to an identity by which people will soon begin to characterize you. "He never has anything good to say about anything or anyone." "Don't bother telling her anything good or bad that's happened to you; she will always have experienced something better or worse."

You may think those statements are judgmental, but a characterization is not the same thing as a judgment. People will form a characterization after experiencing regular interactions with a person. If you are called a "Debbie downer" after someone meets you for the first time, you are being judged. If someone interacts with you multiple times over a few months and then characterizes you that way, you would do well to take an honest look at how often you focus on the negative.

If you've created a limiting social identity via a negative coping behavior, you may want to take deliberate steps to catch and correct it. Exercise self-awareness so that you recognize critical, sarcastic, or demeaning behavior as you are doing it. Correcting involves an immediate action to stop that behavior. The best correcting actions are reflecting and apologizing.

American novelist and poet Nancy Willard wrote, "Answers are closed rooms; and questions are open doors that invite us in."[9] That statement certainly applies to social relationships, but asking yourself questions about what you hoped to gain through a particular action is essential to the EI practice of reflecting. Like finding a new way to get from your home to your favorite restaurant, insights from self-reflective questions help you discover less harmful ways to meet your interpersonal needs.

Apologizing is the quickest way to end and self-correct a negative social coping behavior. You don't need to make a big deal out of it. If you catch yourself being sarcastic, just stop and say, "I'm sorry I shouldn't be insulting in an attempt to be funny." Will it humble you a bit? Yes. But stopping that automatic negative behavior will require some humility and apologizing also sets up some informal accountability, which is never a bad thing. Negative social coping behaviors harm your existing relationships and set up barriers to new ones. It would be wise to make whatever efforts you can to remove those identity hats for good.

growing your social skills

As digital communication overtakes face-to-face interaction, good social skills become much harder to develop. Using texts, email, social media posts, and emojis offers convenience and helps a lot of socially uncomfortable people stay engaged. However, relying on those forms of communication does not prepare us for interaction in groups of people or for situations which require face-to-face communication. What I'm saying is that we, as a society, must focus on improving our socialization skills as a counterbalance to our growing dependency on digital communication. Your EI growth might benefit from evaluating whether the identity hat you wear is promoting healthy socialization or keeping you from connecting well by limiting how people respond to and interact with you. Let me share a couple of social development practices that have helped me in face-to-face communication.

watch for cues

People will tell you a lot without saying a word. The challenge is you can get so wrapped up in what you are trying to communicate that you fail to notice what they are communicating. Pull your focus away from yourself and what you are saying so you can observe the subtle cues the other person is sending. If you see them wince or widen their eyes, stop and make an adjustment by saying something like, "Wait, I don't think that came across in the way I meant it," then rephrase what you said, or ask them what they heard.

Remember that everything always sounds better in your head than it does when you say it out loud. It sounds good to you because you use your own language, humor, and approach to the subject. Without that context, the people listening to you may have some reaction of agreement, disagreement, confusion, or surprise. Make it your goal to learn something from every interaction, and you will grow significantly in your conversation skills.

leave conversational breathing space

Like the lady I described earlier, you might be trying to alleviate your personal discomfort by filling up all the dead space with words. I find myself doing this from time to time. My response to a single question will be detailed, usually connected to two other random but related things, and always long.

While you should not merely give yes and no answers, you do want to leave room for others to ask follow-up questions or to contribute their thoughts about the subject. Dead space in conversations can be unnerving. But speaking from my experience, I know that sometimes I don't have an immediate response to what someone else just said. I need a moment to formulate a reply or contribution. The person you are communicating with may need that space as well.

get curious

In my training as a professional academic life coach, I learned the value of curiosity. To respect the client's thoughts and priorities, I have to set aside where I think they *should* go and simply follow them. The best way to do that is to remain curious about what they are saying. Why did they use that word to describe what happened? What is most important to them about the decision they made? These kinds of questions have transformed situations I used to absolutely dread, namely, "airplane chatter." Now I can have enjoyable conversations with strangers.

Emotional intelligence is not only about your self-awareness and identifying and managing your own emotions. It applies to social awareness too. Making the effort to notice the coping behaviors you use to relate to others and discerning what they may be experiencing and feeling will greatly improve your social interactions. This will take some practice to be sure, but the payoff in lower anxiety and higher enjoyment in your socialization will be well worth the attention you give it.

CHAPTER NINE

ordinary
paper trash

Paper trash is probably what you think of when I use the term *litter*. Containers and napkins from fast-food restaurants, receipts, pages from school or work projects, candy wrappers, tissue paper from gift bags or the kind that catches nasal discharge. Paper of all sorts ends up trapped against median walls or hanging in the branches of roadside foliage. More than anything else, it is this kind of litter that triggers the desire to find who to blame, which is not unjustified. Some people willfully throw trash out onto the side of the road, and they should be held responsible for that action.

We should, however, allow for the possibility that the littering was accidental. It has happened to me. Driving along with the windows down on a nice spring day, my eye caught a paper napkin floating up into my rearview mirror. For a moment it reminded me of those zero-gravity planes that, by their rapid ascent and descent patterns, create a few seconds of anti-gravity where people and items float around outside the gravitational pull of the earth.

I checked my speedometer and recognized that the napkin was not defying gravity but was caught in the circular wind movements caused by the open windows. It was kind of a magical moment, seeing this object floating while my car was moving down the highway at seventy miles per hour. Suddenly I was jarred away from this dreamy state as the paper caught the outside edge of the current which then ripped it from the car. Now, further out in my rearview mirror, I'm seeing my trash drifting, tumbling, spinning, and tossing on its way down to the pavement.

As often as we see (or participate in) accidental roadside littering, there are likely more times when we have seen careless people toss trash out their window, driving away with no regard for what they leave blowing and tossing in the wind, adding to the debris that collects on the side of the road. They seem to be clueless that what they've discarded will become someone else's job to clean up. Perhaps it's not cluelessness as much as carelessness. They toss trash out the window of their car without care.

carelessness

I have an ear that catches the misuse of phrases. I don't go around telling people how they are saying something incorrectly; it all just goes on in my head. One of my favorite things to do is listen to how people respond when they are asked specific questions. On the History Channel's show *Pawn Stars*, the staff of the pawn shop regularly brings in experts to help them determine the authenticity or value of objects. Their question to the customer typically is, "Do you mind if I call in an expert to take a look at this?" Nine of ten people respond, "Sure, that would be great." But by saying "Sure," they are in fact saying "Yes, I do mind you calling someone."

Another phrase that gets regularly misused is "I could care less." The phrase is supposed to be "I *couldn't* care less," which indicates that their capacity to care about something is at rock bottom. The incorrect version in fact says they *do* care, and that there are levels of uncaring beyond the care they presently have. I know you may be thinking "you poor sick man" about now. Yep.

People tend to use "I could care less" to defend their uncaring actions or dismissive attitude toward a problem or person.

The careless act of throwing trash out of your car is not the casual type of carelessness we might use to describe, for example, a person who is not careful with money. In that instance, we are saying the person doesn't pay close attention to money and spends it haphazardly.

Carelessness in its primary definition means that a person lacks care. A lot of us do that: we stop caring about the way that our actions impact others. The carelessness of littering creates a dirty and unpleasant environment for everyone else who drives down the same road or shares the same space, perhaps especially for those who are asked or compelled to pick up the trash we leave behind.

Pamela and I enjoy camping in our small pop-up trailer. Sometimes that enjoyment is interrupted when we show up at our reserved camp site and find that the people who used it in the days before we arrived, left a mess. Before we can enjoy the camp site, we have to clean up half-burned trash in the fire pit, candy wrappers strewn about, and spilled food drying on the picnic table. We try to be careful to leave campsites cleaned up and ready for the next group, but I know there are other places in my life where people are picking up after me.

At the other extreme, caring about what I do and how it affects others can lead to people pleasing. This can be a deep trap as you make failed attempts to keep everyone around you happy. It won't happen; it's just not possible.

The vital center of that scale asks you to be honest with yourself by recognizing that there are byproducts of your activity. Your physical presence, the things you use, the wrappers from your fast food, your impulsively spoken words, the things you claim to be and don't end up being—these all are a part of the waste materials of your life. There is no shame in this byproduct. It's human. It's natural.

You know where the problem lies, right? It's in failing to clean up after yourself. If you produce debris in a place where other people will travel, pick it up before you move on. Just paying attention to and cleaning up the waste material of your life can vastly improve the environment for others who share the road with you. Backpackers say it simply: "Pack your trash!" Let me offer a couple of personal clean-up strategies that are easy to implement but can make a big difference.

clean up after hard conversations

Everyone has conversations that get raw, honest, and sometimes angry. They are necessary from time to time to keep the truth present in our minds and relationships. Don't make the mistake of leaving the debris of these difficult conversations floating around like paper thrown out a car window. You accelerate away from the exchange in hopes that things will become normal again in a few days. Sometimes they do, but even when they appear normal, you find yourself having to step around debris still lying on the pavement.

Cleaning up after a hard conversation means honoring the relationship enough to circle back after a few hours or perhaps a day and make sure the other person is OK. Ensure that you understood what they said and apologize for things spoken in a moment of pain or pride. It's helpful to wait long enough for things to cool down but not so long that the relationship turns cold and indifferent.

watch your interruptions

Being with people can create the energy to compare, compete, or prove ourselves in the opinions of others. Meaningful conversations need breathing space. Often, people do not receive the gift of patience as they tell their stories. One of the most honoring actions you can take in a conversation is to assume the role of interviewer. "So, you said you were really embarrassed by what happened. What was embarrassing about it?" "What do you wish you had done differently?" "How do you feel about that person now that some time has gone by?"

In a recent Interpersonal Workplace Relationships workshop, I asked the participants to practice pausing and asking one follow-up question for every statement someone made in their conversations over the following few days. Two days later, I received an email from one of the organizers. He shared how he used that practice in a dinner meeting the night before with a good friend. He remarked at how great their conversation had been, and he recognized how asking follow-up questions had made his friend feel listened to and valued.

Sadly, interruptions have become a tolerated part of our discourse. I want to be heard and noticed. I want people to pay attention to and listen to me. I'd be ashamed to count the times I've been guilty of cutting people off in the middle of their stories so I could tell mine. For me, interruptions are a type of waste matter typically generated by my need to be known or noticed or to hide my insecurities. This kind of conversational debris clutters relational spaces and detracts from their enjoyment.

stay aware of the equilibrium of needs

Our cultural focus has turned decidedly toward individualism and the right to be who and what a person wants. This naturally leads to disregard for others. You can become oblivious to the impact that "being you" and securing what you need has on others. When your needs become so important that they push the needs of others out of consideration, you end up littering the roadway with the debris of self-centeredness. Entitlement works directly against your growth in Emotional Intelligence, and it makes travel less enjoyable for everyone else.

In the next chapter, I'll explore the idea that communities have their own ecosystems. The balance of give and take must be preserved, or the system will begin to break down. That ecosystem also includes the balance of needs. If you equalize the attention to your needs with the needs and concerns of others, you will add to the strength and wellness of your relationships. The healthy function of community includes the action of looking out for each other. Regard for others—noticing and tending to their needs—communicates you care and value them in a powerful way.

CHAPTER TEN

life vests

If you travel roads that lead to recreational lakes and campgrounds, you will often see items that have blown out of boats. Bright orange life vests are common debris along these routes. Made of buoyant material, they are necessarily lightweight but also susceptible to the currents blowing through the open bow of a trailered boat.

Whenever I see a life vest lying in the highway median, I can't help but remember Bill Murray playing a psychiatric patient in the 1991 movie *What about Bob?*[10] Due to his extreme fear of water, he tries to overcome it lashed to the mast of a sailboat with ropes, happily repeating, "I'm sailing. . . I'm a sailor. . . I sail. . ."

Many people see the bright orange life vest Bob is wearing but don't notice that he has two more strapped to each of his legs.

No one really enjoys wearing life preservers. Most adults won't wear them while riding in a boat, but boat operators are legally required to have one present and available for every passenger. And in all fifty states, laws dictate that children ages twelve and younger must wear them at all times. Apart from the trouble you could have with law enforcement on the lake, and the uncomfortable and conspicuous feeling you may have while wearing a life vest, the loss of one could be catastrophic if there's an accident out on the open water.

I recently noticed a life vest caught against a wire fence along the highway near my home. The sight caused me to jot down these questions: What are my life preservers? Have they gone missing? What helps preserve my life when I'm off the road and in deep water?

I asked these self-awareness questions to help identify what or who helps me thrive, especially when going through difficult or overwhelming times. Life preservers can be activities as well as people. Let's explore activities first.

life-preserving activities

You may get too busy or distracted to keep up on the kinds of activities that feed your soul. Compounding the problem, you may not make the connection back to the element you're missing.

One night a few months ago, I had a profound realization while standing in the pale glow of the open refrigerator door. As I scanned the shelves for something to eat, I wondered, "What am I doing?" I realized I was feeling low on energy, so I was hunting for something sugary and preferably chocolatey to perk me up. I squinted to see the green numbers on the microwave clock: 11:52 p.m. Most people were in bed, having realized that the fatigue they felt, and their stone-heavy eyelids were signs that they should get some rest. I was misinterpreting those indicators and instead searching for stimulants.

That type of misinterpretation will keep you gasping for air and struggling to survive when you are dogpaddling in deep water. The life preserver blew out of the boat and is now somewhere in the bushes lining the highway. But you're not thinking about the life vest; you're thinking about food, or romance movies, or sex, or white sand beaches and bottles of beer, or lime margaritas and decadent desserts. And you're lying to yourself about time. "I just need to get through this demanding couple of weeks and then things will be better." "Tomorrow will have to be better because today is the worst it could be." Entertaining false hope about time and using stimulants and distractions are numbing agents to lessen the anxiety of drowning.

Save yourself by making a clear connection to what's gone missing. Some activity life preservers may be regular intervals of solitude, exercise (that you truly enjoy), or the singular and easy focus that accompanies hobbies such as cooking, gardening, or playing an instrument. These activities are part of your self-care and typically the first things to go missing when your life's waterline rises with the demands of work, family, health, and finances. Do whatever you need to do to keep your life-preserving activities active.

life-preserving people

The concept of people as life preservers gets a little complicated, mainly because the weight of an entire human being is tough for anyone to bear (and no, I'm not just referring to body weight). But that doesn't keep people from trying to save others, and it may explain why some people disappear from our lives. When one person feels responsible for saving the life of another, there is an initial rush of, shall we call it, saviorhood. It propels them to provide unlimited time, empathy, support, and care. After a while, though, the savior burns out and feels in jeopardy of drowning. Coroners cite a specific cause of death when someone dies while trying to save someone else from drowning: Aquatic Victim Instead of Rescuer (AVIR) Syndrome.[11] In the victim's panic to push down on something to keep their head above water, they end up pushing the rescuer under.

So how do you keep human life preservers in the boat? I suggest that you think about your relationships in terms of a village or tribe as opposed to a single savior. Having a few healthy relationships allows you to fall into over-your-head waters from time to time and find several hands to help you out. There will always be certain people who are able to help when you are struggling in terms of time and energy. They may also be connected to you in a way that puts them on the front line. By forging and cultivating a larger group of friends, you are acting to preserve your preservers. Those who have rescued you alone on multiple occasions or over the course of long periods of time, will tend to burn out and then drift out of your life.

It's also important to stay aware of the giving-receiving balance in your tribe. Communities have their own ecosystems. The interdependence of an ecosystem requires that you participate in rescuing others as well as being rescued. If you do not cultivate empathy, you will lack focus to see where others need help. If you do not live sacrificially and offer the availability to step up, you will truncate the healthy functioning of the ecosystem and cause it to fragment. However, if you tend to that balance and invest yourself by giving empathy and energy within your tribe, you will find more than enough help when you are struggling to keep your head above water.

life preservers outside of the water

I've made a couple of references to prayer throughout these pages, and while I'm not pushing religion here, I feel compelled to make one clear connection to matters of faith. Remember what I mentioned earlier about the weight of human beings? You have the ordinary weight of being a person with roles, responsibilities, and practical challenges. In addition to that weight, you have what you might call mystical weight. Questions about existence and non-existence, meaning and purpose, suffering and injustice all contribute to the conundrums and mysteries that press lightly on your psyche on some days and heavily on others. As long as humans have walked this planet, they have looked outside the natural realm of beings also stuck to the ground by gravity and reached for answers to these mysteries in the something, or someone beyond.

The biblical writer in the Book of Ecclesiastes differentiates those who live under the sun from the existence of one who lives above it.[12] There is validity in questioning whether people (who suffer from the same limitations and confinements of living under the sun) can answer these great mystical questions or help ease the burdens they impose on our souls. And for all human history, the resounding answer to that question seems to be "they cannot."

A few years ago, I attended a conference at which a speaker shared a story about driving across a bridge in Washington state. As he caught a glimpse of the river rushing below, he noticed that there were people in the cold winter water, so he pulled over to see what was going on. Leaning over the bridge, he saw a few people standing on the side of the river and two others in wetsuits on surfboards, bouncing up and down on the churning water. The "surfers" had tied ski ropes to the bridge supports, which allowed them to remain in fixed spots, and were having a great time riding the current rushing beneath their boards.

He noted that had the surfers been attached to anyone in the water, they would likely have been in a mutual crisis, being swept together downstream in the rain-swollen rapids. The thing that transformed this from crisis to recreation was attaching the ski ropes to an immovable structure outside the river.

This observation impacted me deeply. His point aligned with what I'm communicating here: something or someone "above the sun" might be the only reliable anchoring point, especially when you are treading the deep waters of mystery and wrestling with questions that transcend the wisdom, strength, and abilities of folks in the water with you.

Thriving requires more than breathing in and out and getting rest and food adequate to keep your body alive. Your life depends on a buoyancy beyond yourself to keep both your head and heart above water. It is the deeper, mysterious part of your heart or soul that must find its life-preserving resources in something or someone above the sun, something or someone outside the common confines of humanity.

This is the realm of faith, belief, and hope. Perhaps you've had these life preservers at earlier points in your life, and yet somewhere along the many miles of your personal highway, they have gone missing. I encourage you to recover your faith and do what you need to do to ensure that the people, practices, and beliefs that help you keep your head above water are traveling securely with you.

CHAPTER ELEVEN

making peace with what is

Many of you see the roadside debris I've talked about, and your first instinct is to find answers for how it got there. "Who's to blame? What can we do to stop the polluters?" I get it. I can't see trash floating in a stream or lying along the road without recalling that iconic image from the 1970s commercial showing polluted landscapes and a Native American man with a tear trickling down his weathered face. Environmental pollution endangers our natural resources. Why shouldn't we figure out how the trash got there and hold someone accountable?

I don't disagree with the anger over the pollution or the desire to find the people responsible for causing it. My point is that your fixation on assigning blame can prevent you from dealing with the reality that the trash is still everywhere on the sides of the road.

The debris piles up, and its existence doesn't change when you figure out who is responsible, why someone dumped it, or how it got there. Life regularly sends you into situations that beg for this kind of explanation. However, I've found that going on an obsessive search for who, why, or how, can prevent you from simply seeing and figuring out a way to *be* with what *is*.

I worked with a consultant for a few months, and an insightful statement he repeatedly said to me was "blame blinds." If you want to see the whole situation (including your part), he said, "You have to stop looking for someone to blame." I didn't like his advice, but it rang true to my experience.

This has true implications around the pollutants you see in your relationships. You may have an angry and uncooperative coworker whose attitude adversely impacts his productivity at work. What's making him that way? Is he drinking too much, going through an ugly divorce, or staying up too late playing video games or watching porn?

Though your evaluation may be accurate, your search for the cause will likely involve some wild guesses. Some of your search for a cause or explanation can be a veiled effort to fix people. "If they would just..." "I wish they would..." "It would be so much easier to work with them if they would only..." Unfortunately, your speculation as an armchair therapist will not significantly change the conditions that exist.

speculative fixing

Somewhere in all that speculation, you stop dealing with the person. You stop relating to them as they are and begin setting expectations for them to be as you want and need them to be. Let's say your spouse is depressed. Your conclusions about how they got there or the seventeen suggestions on how they can get out of it (which you found using a Google search) will not change the emotional malaise in which they awaken every day.

Your son is unmotivated, your supervisor is disillusioned by his job, the person driving ahead of you is distracted and clueless. On and on it goes. Using labels, finger pointing, the shaking your head in exasperation most often will lead to a frustrating dead end. You may find the situation responsible or accurately diagnose why someone is the way they are, but you're still left dealing with the ongoing, persistent reality of what *is*.

A friend was mentoring a young man in his early twenties named Blake. Blake also participated in a group of young adults my wife and I were guiding through a process of personal and career development. As we (mentors) sat down for coffee one day, my friend and I both expressed frustration that Blake had come to a sticking point and wasn't showing signs of forward movement. I vented, "If he would just face up to his fear of losing his father's approval, he would be so much further down the road by now."

My conclusion was valid. I had identified a significant part of the personal restriction Blake was facing which clouded his judgment regarding his career path. I had concisely diagnosed the problem and prescribed the solution. Dr. Witt had stepped in and done his job. Take the medicine and be happy.

My friend interrupted the satisfaction I was enjoying with my life-changing recommendation by repeating my first four words back to me. "Yeah," he said. "If he would just. . ."

I knew exactly what he meant. It's so easy to give a "just face up to that fear" recommendation, but Blake's fear was entangled in complex thoughts, emotions, and relationships. My simple prescription minimized them. "Just" did not address the family history, culture, expectations, and relationship dysfunction which were directly contributing to his complex situation.

Through a lot of interactions with people like Blake, I've had to resign myself to the fact that people don't need to be fixed as much as they need supporters who figure out a way to be with them until they can find their own way forward. I've found that figuring that out is much better for me too.

how to *be* with what *is*

The problems, pain, and dysfunction in others does impact you. You may find yourself vacillating between feeling genuinely sorry for them at one point and then boiling over in anger at other points. Dealing with constant negativity, anxiety, sarcasm, anger, attention-seeking, indecisiveness, complaining, or passive-aggressive behaviors in others can overwhelm. The personal debris piles up, and, like roadside trash, it makes traveling together (living with or around others) less enjoyable.

It would be much better if the polluted conditions in the lives of others were cleaned up. It would seem reasonable that it would be better for them, and certainly, it would be better for you. I'm sure you've wasted a ton of energy—as I have—trying without success to get people to see how their behaviors are impacting themselves and others. And encouraging them to adapt, change, improve, or move forward.

At some point, for the sake of sanity if nothing else, you'll want to stop fixating on fixing your family, friends, neighbors, supervisors, or coworkers. You don't have a magic wand to wave, and the fruitless pursuit of finding blame or prescribing fixes becomes emotionally exhausting. What if, instead, you put your attention on determining whom or how *you* need to be so that you can deal with life situations and people in them *as they are*? What would it take for you to be content with what *is*? What kind of person would you need to become to live with the tensions, frustrations, and disappointment if change for someone else comes slowly or not at all?

Adaptability is a primary characteristic of people with high Emotional Intelligence. People with low EI tend to keep the expectations on the circumstances or individuals around them instead of making personal adaptations. Your mental and emotional wellbeing require regular adjustments to ensure that your contentment isn't primarily based on the actions or inactions of others.

who will you need to become?

In my coaching practice, I try to help the client in three areas: seeing, being, and doing. Seeing means exploring and understanding a larger picture of their situation, options, and perspectives. This part of coaching is relatively easy if the client is ready to work and think with me about their life. Creating realistic and yet challenging actions (the *doing* part of this triad) comes relatively easy with most of my clients. The greatest challenge I find in coaching is helping the client understand who they are and what kind of person they will need to become to move forward.

You sabotage most of the changes you want to make personally by not addressing the kind of person you are (your being) in two areas: accurately understanding the kind of person you have been and how that way of being has contributed to where you are.

Life remains as it is when you make endless excuses, procrastinate, avoid, fail to plan, and make your decisions dependent on the actions of others. Until you connect the dots between the way you have been to the results of that way of being, you will likely continue those behaviors. And experience the same results.

The second area is understanding the kind of person you will need to become in order to move into the future you want. In the same way that an athlete works on a specific part of their abilities to compete at a higher level, your personal development in specific areas will give you the capacity to live happier and stronger when faced with difficulties. This is particularly important in relation to unchangeable people or circumstances.

Rutger Bregman in his book *Humankind—A Hopeful History* gives nearly 500 pages of evidence to support his central thesis that, at our roots, humans are "friendly, peaceful, and healthy."[13] I don't disagree entirely with the premise, but I do believe that otherwise friendly, peaceful, and healthy people experience traumas, get trapped in unhealthy mindsets, suffer mental disorders, and live in protracted social and emotional dysfunctions. These obstacles all contribute to ways of thinking and acting that counterbalance that positive view of humanity.

The danger in holding too much hope in humanity is in falling victim to false optimism. False optimism believes if you just try a little harder, apply a bit more pressure, set an ultimatum, go the extra mile, up the ante, or whatever other self-determined efforts you can imagine doing, that a specific person or situation will change. I'm not saying these efforts are always futile. I'm suggesting that, in some instances, no amount of energy, tactics, reasoning, blood, sweat, or tears—yes even tears—will make any significant difference.

In most instances, our unchangeable circumstances involve an organization which we can't quit, or, more painfully, they involve people from whom we cannot simply walk away. What does it mean then to personally grow and become a certain kind of person so that you can better live with unchangeable people and circumstances? You can try a couple of tactics based on what I've seen people do who are able to live with what *is*.

set and keep boundaries

You won't gain much ground into the territory of changing people's personal behaviors, but you can determine how far these behaviors intrude into yours. People who desire things in their lives to remain as they are, often create hoops for you to jump through or conditions which can hold you emotionally hostage.

A lady approached me after a workshop I conducted, tearfully explaining how she could not be honest with her adult daughter about the deep concerns she had over the daughter's new boyfriend. When I asked why she felt that way, she said, "The last time I questioned her decision, which was over something as impersonal as a lease she was signing on an apartment, she cut off all communication with me for nearly two years."

Now, I don't know all the history in this relationship, but it's apparent the daughter is training her mother how to be with her. The mother could be a part of the daughter's life, but she does not get to question any of her decisions.

A handful of people in your life will attempt to do that with you too. They will resort to emotional manipulation, accusing you that you don't really love or support them, and blaming you for their current problems. They will use money, their children, your contact with the children, and anything else that matters to you to get you to let them live as they want to live. I know it looks evil, but in most cases, they are doing what they feel they must do to keep their life together. It doesn't make much sense, but the actions of people living in pain and self-protection seldom do.

You need to know where your lines and limits are. Saying, "I will do this, but I won't do that" will likely get a reaction from the people who want accommodation for their unwillingness to change. You can't prevent this, but growing in your ability to set and maintain personal boundaries will help you live stronger and happier with people who fiercely resist change.

grow your empathy

I find that most people confuse empathy with sympathy. Sympathy identifies with a person's problems usually with a strong desire to bring immediate comfort. A sympathetic response will have you trying to restore the individual to a state of happiness as quickly as possible. We should offer sympathy to victims of accidents, those agonizing over the loss of a family member, or to those diagnosed with a life-threatening disease. Addicts, bigots, and others who are extremely interested in keeping their life as is love sympathizers.

There are usually deep and complex reasons keeping a person stuck in their pain or problems. From your outside perspective, assumptions about what they could or should do to move through their depression, end toxic relationships, or press forward with abandoned goals can appear obvious and simple. Empathy gives you glimpses of how the world looks through the eyes of another person. It provides context, helping you understand more of what they are facing and what's involved in their actions or inactions. Healthy empathy does not feel compelled to rush in and make things better.

Your ability to see the situation through their eyes is, as I introduced it, is an empathetic glimpse. When you see lack of effort on their part, like I did with Blake, it can appear that your interest in their improvement is greater than theirs. Take notice where your concern for them is being replaced with disappointment in them. This indicates that you might need to reacquaint yourself with the way life looks from their vantage point.

This is a place of becoming (development of personal growth) that will require regular reinforcement, but it will be well worth the effort. Seeing briefly through their eyes helps you, patiently and without judgment, find proactive ways to support them rather than writing them off.

lower and longer expectations

Maintaining expectations of people who show no evidence of changing their behaviors will pull you down emotionally and mentally. They keep doing what they've always done, and you keep holding on to the ideal that they'd be so much better off if they would start making better or wiser choices. Without a change on one side of that equation or the other, you will experience an ongoing internal disruption.

I regularly experience waking up with my mind spinning like it has been hard at work while I've been sleeping. No one enjoys waking up feeling brain-tired, like you've already ran a mental marathon. The repeated disappointment in the behavior of others can create that kind of mental fatigue. You run through multiple scenarios of how they could be making progress if only they would make different choices. You may even find yourself in an ongoing state of anxiety by catastrophizing the outcomes of their behaviors. To live well emotionally and mentally with change-averse people, you simply must adjust your expectations to lower levels or longer timelines.

managing you

Wisdom tells us that we can only manage ourselves. Seeking to control situations or people is a shortcut to exasperation. When you make the choice to stop blaming, asking the elusive questions of who, why, and how, you are free to decide how you're going to *be* with what *is*. In the end, it's much more productive than your efforts at fixing others or trying to get them to be someone other than who they are. Pushing away from assumptions, impatience, and blame allows you to redirect your life energy to the way you are managing your own emotions, thoughts, and actions.

You may not like how things are and would prefer something very different, but this is what *is*. Often, figuring out how to *be* with what you cannot immediately change provides the healthiest and most empowering solution.

CHAPTER TWELVE

adopt-my-highway

During the time of my research and planning for this book, I came across a website created by Loui Tucker.[14] For over sixteen years, Loui, her wife Sabine, and other volunteers have regularly cleaned up debris along a traffic-clogged section of Interstate 280 near her home in San Jose, California. Her website (louitucker.com) caught my attention because she keeps track of both the volume and type of trash that they have collected along this two-and-a-half mile stretch of highway since 2006.

I called Loui and asked if I could interview her. She agreed, and we had an enjoyable hour-long conversation about how she got involved in this Adopt-a-Highway effort. Loui is a "stop complaining and do something" sort of individual. I really like that about her. Businesses will often adopt a section of highway, but many just hire a contractor to do the cleanup work. They gain the positive publicity of having their name on a sign that is seen by millions of travelers and commuters and then write off a nice annual tax deduction.

Loui is one of a growing number of individuals who complete the Caltrans training and receive a five-year permit to clean specific sections of California highways. Caring for the environment and an ambition of just "keeping things clean" motivate her. Unlike corporation-funded cleanups, Loui takes the time to separate the waste debris from items that can be recycled and other items that can be cleaned up and donated.

She and Sabine have a mission to repurpose stuffed animals they find on their assigned stretch of highway. Every year, they salvage dozens of grimy discarded toys, cleaning and repairing them. Many of these stuffed toys have found a home in their spare bedroom. Once a year they pick out a dozen or so stuffed animals and give them to the fire department. The station keeps them on hand to give to children who have been burned out of their home and lost everything.

Some of Loui's responses to my questions in the interview prompted the suggestions I'd like to offer here in these closing pages. These suggestions relate to areas of roadside cleanup on your personal and relational highways. From my experience working with individuals and groups, it is important that we make positive decisions which keep the lanes of connection with others clear of hazards and debris. Let's call it "Adopt-My-Highway" and explore ways to keep interpersonal relationships cleaned up and healthy.

clean-up in community

Keeping a two-and-a-half mile stretch of highway clean without some additional help proved challenging, so through the years, Loui and Sabine have invited others to help with the cleanup. They've made these invitations through organizations like volunteermatch.org or local high school Key Clubs.

On one cleanup day, twenty teenage volunteers joined them. Loui quickly realized that "I couldn't do that anymore. That was just not feasible." Managing volunteer groups presents unique challenges, like managing the different motivations that bring volunteers to the event. Many times, volunteers are just looking for the experience or to check off a box of community service. Over the years, Loui has found that she prefers to work with a regular group of similarly motivated adults from an email list she maintains. As difficult as organizing people can be, there's no way one or two people can keep up with the cleanup task. Developing relationships and working together in community is difficult, but community is vital.

peopling

We need people. Living together with others enriches our lives. Successfully getting through challenges in life depends on the relationships you build and bring with you into the future. Your personal needs for companionship may be less than others require, but everyone has them. Sometimes relationships are messy, and you likely don't have all the tools you need to navigate them well. Additionally, some people have so much personal debris in their lives that they can't hold up their end of a healthy relationship.

Perhaps you made close friends easily when you were in high school and then, moving forward in life, you assumed that it would still be easy. You waited for it to happen again. And you waited. Some of you may have waited so long that you gave up, assuming that there were no people around you who were worth having as friends. You decided that a close-knit community of people was just not going to be part of your life.

Friendships do take a greater investment of energy and time to develop than they ever have. Long before the COVID-19 pandemic, Americans were increasingly becoming socially isolated. We could list a couple dozen cultural and economic reasons for the friendship deficiency, but I'm not sure how that helps. There are actions you can take, however, to increase your chances of finding and building healthy community.

relationship discernment

First, take a deeper look at the relationships you've had that worked and those which did not. Can you discern your part in succeeding or failing to keep them long term? What needs are you seeking to meet through those relationships? Someone seeking approval may end up manipulated and hurt by so-called friends because their need obscures warning signs that the person is not trustworthy. Recognize the debris of unrealistic expectations, not trusting others, or approval-seeking to the point that you stop being yourself. These are hazards on the road to healthy relationships, so you would do well to acknowledge those areas and do some clean up.

I hope some of the ideas we've explored through metaphors in this book might prove helpful with your "Adopt-My-Highway" project. I've encouraged the practice of reflection a few times in these pages. Everyone needs quiet, distraction-free time to think deeply and carefully about life amidst the swamp of non-stop noise and movement. This practice is especially important for you to see the core elements that make a relationship work versus relationships that are "working" you.

invite, invite, invite

Second, I strongly encourage you to open time on your calendar to invite people into your life or to go out and see them, even if you do this only once or twice a month. In an interview I read, an Amish leader was asked about the exclusion of TV and radio among their community. His answer was: "(These things) would destroy our visiting practices. We would stay at home with television or radio rather than meet with other people. How can we care for the neighbor if we do not visit with them or know what is going on in their lives?"[15] Indeed, how can we?

And just a head's up. . . you may have to invite and reinvite people into your life or activities until you experience invitation fatigue. I recently saw a Facebook exchange between two Millennial moms. They expressed frustration about having made plans with people—weddings and other events that cost money, along with casual events such as dinners and game nights—only to have the invitees opt out via text at the last minute or just not show up.

This is a significant phenomenon. Event organizers must now over-invite, sometimes by 50 to 70 percent, to account for the people who say they will attend but don't show up. You may face this too, leading to invitation fatigue. Keep pressing forward. Go the extra mile because flakiness and low commitment typically do not reflect on you or what you are inviting them to do. It has become a cultural practice where people allow themselves to decide what they are into doing and what they aren't in the very moment they should be leaving to go to the event. They make that impulsive decision without consideration for the people who put valuable time and energy into the invitations. Such selfish and inconsiderate behavior happens so widely and pervasively now that it's become normalized.

Your temptation may be to write people off who leave you hanging, ghost your communication, or take four days to get back to you. As I said, this is a dominant cultural norm, and many people are merely complying with it. I assure you that you will gain some good, strong friendships, but you will need to be persistent and refuse to give up on people after the first couple of last-minute opt-outs. Now, if you are on instance number thirty-two of this kind of behavior, you may need to fish in different waters, but don't give up on fishing.

frequent forgiving

The two previous suggestions have to do with finding friendships. Building and maintaining the community you find, includes one difficult and yet regularly required practice: forgiving. If there was a ranking on advice that was easiest to give and hardest to do, forgiving others would be at or near the top of that list.

There's no need for me to rehearse the benefits you gain by forgiving others. That research is well-documented and widely available, along with a myriad of suggestions on how to navigate that difficult path. For many of you, however, knowing the mental, emotional, and even physiological benefits of forgiving is insufficient to overcome your resistance to do it when faced with the pain and anger of being offended or mistreated. In my personal experience, and through the times I've spent helping people who have been hurt or offended, I've discovered one important mindset shift that can provide significant progress in your movement toward being forgiving.

avoid creating villains

Normal injuries enter our lives through normal people who are acting and reacting in accordance with their personal pain, stubborn self-interest, and brokenness. This reality is summed up in the phrase "Hurt people hurt people." Not one of us are free from the possibility of being affected by the intended or unintended pain caused by others. And none of us can claim innocence of causing pain and harm of our own. That truth should make us more gracious and forgiving, but we tend to have short memories of our own trespasses and remember those done by others for a long, long time.

Keeping your sustained attention on the wrongful actions of others without finding a way to move on tends to produce vilification. As you think about what was done to you and talk to others about it, the severity of the wrong done by the offending person grows and any goodness that might have been found in their character shrinks. Magnified offenses grow quickly in size and severity... "After the way they lied to me, I can tell you that not a single word they say to anyone should be trusted... ever!"

Once you begin vilifying, however, people become easy to dehumanize where you no longer care what happens to them. You just want them to go away, disappear, or get what they deserve.

Think of the last action movie you watched. The portrayal of the deranged villain within the first few minutes sets up the psychological justification for the revenge that the hero ultimately and catastrophically brings down on them. I'm not a person who gets easily angered or is given to violence, so it caught me by surprise once when I leaned over and whispered in my wife's ear, "That man needs to die right now!" We were thirty minutes into watching an action movie at the theater. I can't remember which movie it was or any details about it, but I distinctly remember how the vilifying of the villain was so thorough that I would have been satisfied to watch him die at thirty-five-minutes into the film, roll the credits, and finish my popcorn in the car on the way home.

Vilification in relationship offenses keeps you from humanizing those who wronged you. Yes, there are villains. There are psychopathic people who feel nothing as they bring incredible harm and pain into the lives of others. Fortunately, they are not the norm.

The norm is made up of people who all aspire for happiness and contentment and yet all suffer in some way. The human condition is defined by this tension and every one of our coping mechanisms from fearful isolation to abusive manipulation are created from it. Please know that this way of viewing others does not condone what they've done or obligate you to endure what they continue to do. I'm suggesting that you can have better relationships and a greater capacity to forgive if you humanize people in their disruptive and hurtful behaviors rather than vilifying them. This is admittedly, a far less optimistic way of viewing the world, and yet it provides a truer way of seeing ourselves and others.

The offenses you experience through the actions of others will require a good measure of self-discipline to resist vilifying them. But in that effort, you can find an empathetic lens through which you see others as ordinary human beings, frustrated dreamers, and fellow sufferers.

owning your part

As vilification limits your empathy, it also limits your capacity for self-insight. Focusing on the horrible actions of others can be a way of letting yourself off the hook for what you contributed to the way things are. I'm not referring to wrongful actions that others did to you as a child or circumstances where you were deprived of choice. Those matters of forgiveness are deep and most often require the help of a therapist or spiritual advisor.

I'm referring to the more ordinary offenses of being overlooked, forgotten, negatively characterized by someone, spoken to in a mean or hateful way, avoided, disrespected, lied to, or lied about. A singular focus on what was done to you can limit your ability to gain insight from situations that are not always so one-sidedly wrong.

A woman worked as an employee for my organization, and her husband volunteered a great deal of time to our mission. When she resigned, both of them got very vocal and critical toward me and started actively recruiting people to join them in jumping ship.

I had the hardest time finding a way to forgive them for what I saw as subversion and disloyalty. As I reflected on the time that led up to her resignation, I had to admit I had been marginalizing them because I was having a hard time seeing a good fit for them in our evolving organization. I needed to honor them by having honest conversations with them about those concerns, but instead I stopped including them. Owning my part helped me stop vilifying them and move on to forgiveness. It also helped me see some unhealthy patterns of relationship neglect that I needed to improve.

Do yourself a favor by cutting off vilifying thoughts and owning your part in relationship offenses. When you're able to make this kind of self-assessment, you're better positioned to empathetically deal with others' wrongful actions and start down the path of forgiveness.

CHAPTER THIRTEEN

cleaning-up expectations

I asked Loui if sixteen years of cleaning up other people's trash had affected how she views humanity. Her answer intrigued me. She differentiated the trash she picks up on the highway from the trash she picks up on evening walks along the surface streets of her neighborhood. I thought that littering was littering no matter where you found the trash.

She commented, "What's on the freeway tends to be more anonymous because it's not left for you [specifically] if somebody just threw it out the [car] window. When somebody takes a piece of trash and sticks it in a bush when there is a trash can just a few feet away, it's more deliberate." She described these offenders as not only irresponsible but also a little bit malicious.

I could tell by the rise in the cadence of her speech that the trash around the neighborhood was more personally offensive to her. She held local litterers in greater contempt than the people tossing fast-food wrappers, empty cigarette packages, and beer cans out the window of their speeding car. It got me thinking through the categories I've created for people. I make allowances for some, and others burn me up. All of that relates to my expectations of how specific individuals should and shouldn't be.

infatuated with immediacy

I'm convinced that the creation of unrealistic expectations is largely the result of our love affair with immediacy. Overnight solutions, delivery of products we ordered a few hours earlier, and what appears to be sudden financial success or fame all contribute to expectations that solutions should come easy and fast.

In my lifetime, the options available at our fingertips have grown exponentially. I remember ordering items from a catalog that would take weeks to arrive, and the catalog was one of maybe three available. (Yes, I am THAT old!) Now, I can compare prices, quality, and reviews across fifty sources and have my choices delivered to my door the next day.

Such quick-serve solutions have created expectations which we then impose on one of the few things you can't have delivered by Amazon: people. Not only do people not ship well, but they also don't move, change, or adapt well.

Impatience with the slow or non-existent pace of change must be mitigated by holding it against the realities of human behavior. People don't change easily or quickly. They promise, attempt, and, in most cases, sincerely want to change, but the truth is change for most human beings comes slowly and with difficulty.

Sadly, many people dismiss that reality and just redouble their efforts to change others, resorting to the use of shame, manipulation, or (most harmful of all) withholding themselves emotionally and physically from the person they are pressuring to change. I believe strongly in the possibility of change and growth in people. I just don't think it happens as quickly as a Fe-dEx delivery or as magically as portrayed in a Hallmark movie.

idealism

The other primary flaw in expectations is idealism. Again, I think this expectation is being fueled by our culture. Social media is flooded with people who present the very best versions of themselves. Whether it is the camera angle, applied filters and *duck-face* poses in images, or exaggerated boasts about what they have or do, it can appear that perfect or near-perfect exists. Along with that influence we have a regular dose of celebrity worship where everything from sports accomplishments to motion-picture performances are hailed as "flawless," "magical," "beyond belief," or "without compare." The celebration of perfection consciously and subconsciously impacts our expectations of life, work, success, and relationships.

You can choose to see these influences from a distance; recognizing that this idealism indeed happens. The greatest value to the decluttering of your soul from disappointed expectations and the attending burden of resentment, however, is to assess where and how this idealism has directly influenced the expectations you have of your life and the people connected to it. It's one thing for me to say idealism is a problem in society and a wholly other thing to identify the way it affects my personal outlook and expectations.

When the ideal is perfect or near perfect, how can your partner, friend, co-worker, boss, children, or parents measure up? If you hold an idealistic expectation for someone in your life and think they don't know it and feel the pressure of it, you are blindly mistaken. Idealism was the issue behind a statement one of my friends once made as she recalled a difficult conversation she had with one of her mentors. She described it as, "She should-ed all over me." The implied connection to excrement did not go unnoticed by me, but neither was the weight I saw behind her eyes as she said it. Idealism is an un-bearable burden for humans to shoulder. It crushes our souls, and damages our relationships in innumerable ways.

Reconfiguring your expectations will require some shifting in your perspective. Here's a couple suggestions on how to do that well:

realistic capacity

Think about people in relationship to their capacity. In a com-parison with perfection, or even near perfection, all of us will fail. Realistic expectations of people need to be made from an honest comparison to their physical, mental, and emotional capacity. I've tried my best to get disorganized people to be or-ganized or to get people whose normal pace is a mosey to pep up and move faster. In almost every attempt I've made to get people to do something that is outside of who they are or how they are hardwired as a person, I've regretted it.

Capacity can seem like a harsh word, but if you imagine it like someone who is moving groceries from their car to the kitchen it might make more sense. A person who is already carrying three full bags of groceries in one hand and a gallon of orange juice in the other is going to struggle to carry anything more. There are natural and circumstantial limits to what people can be or do. This is another negative to cultural idealism. We are fond of promoting the idea that people can do whatever they imagine; that their potential is limitless. While it may be good to encourage that belief in children (I say "may be," because I don't believe the science supports this blanket affirmation), the reality is everyone has a limited capacity.

It is far more important for us to recognize limitations in others and recalibrate our expectations than to take up the mission of helping people see the limitations in themselves. Expectations that are based on the idea that "Well, I did it, so they should be able to as well" are typically created as a comparison to an idealized version of ourselves. That notion brings to mind the old-timer's line about walking 15 miles to school, barefoot, in the snow, uphill, in both directions.

I went back to school to finish my undergrad studies when I was twenty-eight. I had just started a new 50+ hour a week job at a window coverings manufacturer, was married, and had three children under the age of five. I've been tempted to compare other new dads to how I lived and what I did during that time. Yet there was a lot more that contributed to that season of my life than pure grit and determination. Pamela was a stay-at-home mom and took care of EVERYTHING related to the care of our children and the household. We had a strong and geographically close support system through family and friends. To this day, my body functions well with five to six hours of sleep, so the three to four hours per night at twenty-eight years old was a physical capacity that is not true of everyone. The college I attended had a strong distance learning program which allowed me to work at my own pace through some subjects. Living 10 minutes from campus allowed me to attend some traditional day and evening classes that I could arrange around my work schedule with employers who were also supportive and flexible.

In those details you see things that were unique to my make up along with multiple other factors that were unique circumstantially. All of that contributed to my capacity in that particular season, so it would be unfair to compare people to me and set expectations for them based on my experience. Some people are very slow readers or have learning disabilities that make reading and study extraordinarily difficult. This factors into their intellectual capacity. Other individuals have physical stamina and energy that never seems to give out. Still others battle ongoing depression or suffer with early life traumas that impact their ability to participate in social or work groups.

I've come to believe that the best and truest way to honor another human being is to view and relate to them as they are. It would be horribly wrong to explain to someone the capacity limits you see in them. But it's not wrong to honestly assess those limitations and use that information to recalibrate who you expect them to be and what you expect them to do.

give up on sense-making

I've found that releasing my need for sense-making has been one adjustment which has most benefited my mental, emotional, and relational health. You can do it too. Give up trying to make sense of things people do. When they behave in ways that don't align with what you think is helpful or wise, your natural response will be to try to figure out why. You might even gather the courage to ask them: "Why did you do that?" You will seldom get satisfactory answers to questions like this because people don't make sense.

One of my favorite short books is *It Was on Fire When I Lay Down on It* by Robert Fulghum, titled from the first chapter in this collection of short stories. Fulghum recounts a news story about firefighters called to rescue a man and extinguish a fire burning in his home. After rescuing the man, the firefighters asked him how the fire had started, and he indicated that his bed had been on fire. When they asked him how the bed had caught fire, his response was that he didn't know: "It was on fire when I lay down on it." Fulghum's response to this story is poignant:

About the man in the burning bed story. As with most of what we see other people do, we don't know why they do it, either. If our own actions are mysteries, how much so others? Why did he lie down on a burning bed? Was he drunk? Ill? Suicidal? Cold? Dumb? . . . I don't know. It's hard to judge without a lot more information. Oh sure, we go ahead and judge anyhow. But maybe if judgment were suspended a bit more often, we would like us more.[16]

In the absence of real information, we draw our own conclusions (also known as judgments) about motives, intentions, and diabolical plans. But this sensemaking is a futile exercise. It only helps to fortify our confusion and resentment because we assume the worst when we try to find a reason people do things that may be mysteries even to themselves.

At another point in the interview with Loui, I had asked her a question about times she wanted to give up. In her response, she pointed to a current stalemate with her Caltrans supervisor. She started out saying, "My current supervisor is being a little. . ." and then caught herself and added, ". . . I hesitate to say anything because I don't know what's going on."

I remember smiling at her self-restraint in negatively characterizing him because of her frustration with the situation.

The admission "I don't know what's going on" provides an off-ramp from the one-way expectations you have about others. Expectation debris will constantly be a road hazard in relationships because they leave only one way for the person to be right... doing what you think they should do.

Fulghum's suggestion about suspending judgment means we stop trying to make sense of what people do, suspend our judgments and work on liking *us* better.

CHAPTER FOURTEEN

separating
the debris

After visiting Loui's website, seeing the photos, and reading about the nearly $2,500 in cash and coins they've collected through the years, I was anxious to ask her about other valuable and odd things she and her volunteers have picked up on the side of the road. In the odd category, she talked about a like-new toilet they found with a pair of large rubber boots placed next to it. The toilet wasn't broken like you'd expect in the event it accidentally fell out of a truck. She said it looked like it had been purposefully carried and placed there with the rubber boots on the shoulder of a freeway... who knows why.

On another cleanup day, they found a five-gallon jug like you'd see atop an office dispensing stand with a couple inches of water in it containing a carrot and what looked like a piece of black coal. Someone had put a sign on the jug that read, "Our first snowman, do not discard." The humor of the melted snowman was enhanced by the irony of being discarded on the side of the road despite the instructions on the attached sign.

Besides the cash, the other items they found among the roadside debris were mainly valuable to the people who lost them. Loui and her volunteers have been able to return a lot of items to grateful owners. Among these items was an Apple ID tag and passport they returned to a man who was working in the US on a visa from somewhere in South America. Another was a couple of thumb drives containing video footage belonging to a noted Olympic swimming coach.

Valuable personal items like these or the nine one-hundred-dollar bills they found out among the freeway trash are scarce. Loui reports that only 8-10% of the items they collect are even recyclable. As you might imagine, most of the highway trash is just that. You won't find the A&E network sending out film crews to follow adopt-a-highway volunteers around like they do the treasure hunters on *Storage Wars*.

worthless trash

It's not so easy to put a percentage on what is valuable, recyclable, or just trash that ends up on the personal and relational roadways of our lives. Items like resentment, prejudice, judgment, negative assumptions, defensiveness, envy-draped comparisons, criticism, regrets, offenses, blame, and hypersensitivity can remain for years in the traveling lane of those who are trying to build or rebuild relationships with you. If they must navigate around too much of this kind of debris, they will likely look for more open spaces in the lives of others. None of those items have any enduring value for you, and they will certainly not help you move toward a happy future personally or professionally.

I know that ridding yourself of critical thoughts or feelings of resentment is not as easy as picking up a fast-food bag containing wadded-up, oil-stained napkins with stale French fries stuck on the bottom and sending it off to the landfill. But I also know that doing nothing does nothing. The old expression "time heals all wounds" is a lie. There is an abundance of help for all those worthless thoughts, attitudes, and emotions. Some people opt for therapy, others choose spiritual remedies, still others read self-help books and confide in friends.

There is no one-size-fits-all solution, so keep working at different ways that could help until you find one that does. Along with your choice of guidance or help, simply pay attention. Notice when people can't speak plainly to you because of your hypersensitivity. Notice when you start to boast about what you have or do to buoy your self-worth against comparison to someone else. Pay attention to your knee-jerk readiness to criticize, demean, or blame. Then after you notice the debris, take one immediate, small step away from it.

I'm convinced that this kind of emotional and attitude debris isn't removed from us as much as we move away from it. Human growth means movement. At some point all those immediate, small steps will have created a sizable distance between the person you have grown to be and the worthless debris you've left behind.

recycled experiences

When individuals conduct the roadside clean-up as opposed to a hired crew, they tend to take more interest in sorting the trash and recycling as much as they can. Recyclables, no longer valuable for their original purpose, offer raw material ready for repurposing into something new.

Your life experiences, both good and bad, fall into this debris category. You can always extract something of value from the experiences of your past. I pointed at this living-and-learning process in the chapter on broken pieces of automobiles. By becoming a student of your own life, you can gain useful material from the debris of your experiences, not in a self-absorbed way of course. Take a wide view to analyze and extract beneficial insights about how you relate to the situations and people around you.

The primary hazard in recycling experiential debris comes from associating positive and negative feelings to a specific person, group, place, or event. Often, people who remember fond childhood experiences with cousins separated by years and miles find getting back together as adults deeply disappointing. As much as you want to relive the same feelings from relationships and environments resembling happier times, realities will usually fall short of expectations.

my mild mistrust of stories

People have regularly encouraged me to use more personal experience stories in my writing and public speaking. But this approach does not mesh with my primary learning style. I enjoy learning concepts and examining philosophical frameworks. Personal stories from teachers tend to bore me. That would explain some of my fondness for metaphors, but these also have a weakness.

Both metaphors and personal stories may cause people to miss the larger concept being communicated if they get stuck on the details. I've received emails about everything from gardening tips to medical facts based on a metaphor or personal story I used to illustrate an idea in a presentation. When they zero in on my lack of deeper understanding of fertilizers or the function of white and red blood cells, it seems that the principle was lost on them.

My general observations of human behavior also make me reluctant to use personal stories in my writing and presentations. Personal storytelling assumes that applying the approach to any situation will replicate results. The people telling their story can imply, "If you just do what I did, you can have what I have."

Whether the storyteller specifically says this or not, listeners can easily make this assumption. In either case, that assumption will seldom be confirmed. No matter what that guy with the white teeth, flanked by models and leaning against an expensive sports car, tells you in the late night informercial, there are far too many variables between his sanitized story and you for his successes to be replicated in your experience.

Your personal history will probably also assume replicated results. Your experiences can provide principle-based realizations about how life and relationships work and what attitudes and behaviors lead to happiness or unhappiness. These principles hold the best raw materials with which you can build something current and new, but you must carefully guard against the assumption that replicating the same conditions, people, and environments from your past will generate the same kind of rewards. If you get too fixated on the particulars of the story (who, what, when, where, and how), you risk missing the parts of the story that are truly recyclable.

I worked with a man who had idealized his early college days, as many of us do. He had been a part of a tight-knit group of social activists who had successfully contributed to positive changes in their community. Now in his early forties, that experience set the unattainable bar of comparison he made to new relationships and groups.

By fixating on the rosy memory of that particular time, group, and situation, he failed to extract the experiential raw material: functioning as a community focused on a common purpose. I tried to help him see how recycling the principles from that time could allow him to create fulfilling and rewarding environments in new contexts and among a new circle of relationships.

the valuable among the debris

Though not often, valuable things do find their way to the side of the road. When Loui recounted the different incidents when they found one-hundred-dollar bills out on the side of the highway ($900 total over several clean up days), she expressed her bewilderment at how that could possibly happen. "Were the bills just laying around in the car? Maybe it could happen that one would be outside of a wallet, but nine?"

We considered the loss of valuable items in the "Cargo Straps" chapter and again when I introduced the subject of grief in "Broken Furniture." Things pass so quickly in and out of your hands today. People used to hold on to possessions for years and would never think about selling them to a stranger on Craigslist or Facebook Marketplace for a few bucks.

Now everything seems replaceable and hardly noticed when something ends up as discarded debris on the side of the road. Not just things, but jobs, homes, neighborhoods, social groups, and even people come and go with such regularity and speed that their value fades and diminishes as their newer, shinier, and more exciting replacements fill your thoughts and lay claim to your emotions.

I know some of you would disagree and posit that your new life with its new stuff and relationships is far better than the one before. I won't argue that point because I'm certain some of you had to leave hostile and toxic people or situations to save your sanity and perhaps even your life.

I'm not addressing losses of necessity as much as losses of neglect. It takes effort to keep meaningful relationships strong, growing, and unhindered by highway clutter. You may have stopped inviting people because your friend was always busy or didn't reciprocate the effort you made as often as you expected. Sometimes relationships experience a subtle shift where conversations are not as easy as before. Or you may feel a point of tension, unsure why it's there. Without the persistence and honesty required on both sides to sort out presumptions, unsettled questions, or misunderstandings, it doesn't take long for tension to become avoidance, and before you know it, you refer to all encounters with that friend in the past tense.

vital relationship roles

As you evaluate relationship debris, consider whether a damaged relationship should be left on the side of the road. In today's culture, people have become too willing to cut their losses and simply move on. Unfortunately, you might do this without considering the implication that all valuable relationships include a role. What functional contribution does each person offer the friendship that supports and enhances the experience of the other? Was that person your confidant? Were you their defender? Did they provide energy and motivation for you to go after your dreams? Were you a sounding board for their ideas or a voice that provoked new ways of thinking?

What role did that person fill in your life? What role did you fill in theirs? If you've written off the loss of valuable people and diminished their absence by adding a few distractions, acknowledge that you've left yourself without one or two vital resources necessary to keep focused, balanced, and growing as a human being. The loss of relationship has also created similar gaps for them.

If you think about it, involvement in each other's lives creates the opportunity for tensions. Since this person knows details about your thoughts, fears, and the (now funny, but potentially illegal) thing you did in the summer of 1994, their deep connection might give you pause. "Do they think less of me because of what they know and are hiding that judgment? Will they use that information against me in the future?" Your kick-them-in-the-butt motivational conversation was well intended and probably what they most needed to hear, but the comparison you made to their mom, ex-boyfriend, or a washed-up celebrity crossed a line you didn't know was there.

Interpersonal relationships get messy because they are personal. The same relational roadways that bring help, support, and resources to the souls of others are also opportunities to injure unknowingly and unintentionally, so they require regular maintenance and clean-up. Did something happen in a crucial relationship that needs to be addressed and repaired?

Building and maintaining valuable relationships requires honest, straightforward conversations and sincere apologies that own the specifics of what you did to cause the offense. A deep commitment to deflect perceived offenses and a readiness to assume the best about a friend also preserves these essential ties. Most of those same functions will be necessary to recover the connections which have atrophied.

The roads we all travel require companionship. Meaningful relationships help you to be better, wiser, and stronger than you could become on your own. Don't neglect the connections you have. Be willing to invest some recovery efforts in those you still need (or who still need you) which have, through neglect or injury, ended up a few miles back on the side of the road.

conclusion

The vital truth I hope you have come to at the end of this road trip is: the way you live with your emotions and with others matters. Your growth in Emotional Intelligence will enrich your life and make it more enjoyable. I appeal to you to do this for the sake of your personal wellbeing, but I'm also appealing you to pursue growth in your EI for the sake of our common community.

My repetitive encouragements to grow your social skills in listening, giving grace, and understanding—even to the point of quitting your pursuit of making sense of what others do—will benefit everyone connected to your life. In the rush of our throw-away society, people need to know they matter. We must do better in honoring and valuing them.

If you think about it, we treat as valuable that which is scarce: diamonds, gold, first-edition books, sports cards, even toys. . . Anything that finds its way onto the supply-and-demand cycle will grow value based on how little there is of it. The one exception to that rule is a human being.

There are a lot of us if you hadn't noticed. People aren't assigned value as a result of limited supply. People possess objective intrinsic value. This means our value exists independent of anyone's attitudes or judgements. Human beings have value by virtue of what they are, not measured by other's esteem.

I once heard someone talking about a friend, and they described him this way: "He had felt no soft rain for a very long time, and he lived in the camp of the truly neglected." Those words gripped me. People regularly live in environments devoid of kind words of encouragement, much less celebration and honor.

I worked for a few years in a small window-coverings business in Santa Cruz, California. A business associate just down the road from our workshop manufactured vertical blinds. One day just before lunch, I stopped by their shop to pick up an order, and they invited me to stay and have a piece of birthday cake. A newer employee was turning twenty-one, so the owner's wife baked a cake and brought it over for a lunchtime birthday celebration. We sang a horrible rendition of "Happy

Birthday to You," and they gave the young man a couple of simple presents as the cake was cut and distributed on plain white paper plates.

A couple minutes later, the young man put down his plate, cupped his hands over his face and walked hurriedly out of the shop. I found out later that he had become overwhelmed from the recognition, an unfamiliar expression of honor for him. In twenty-one years, his birthday had never been celebrated. Until he moved out at age seventeen, his alcoholic parents used his birthday as their excuse to party. He had never received a gift, a homemade birthday cake, or off-key singing—just selfish, self-indulgent people drinking themselves into a stupor on the day he should have been celebrated.

Every day other travelers accompany you who have "felt no soft rain for a very long time." They need to know they matter. This goes deeper than just ordinary kindness. Our communities need people who notice others and offer words of encouragement and affirmation. Despite what they do, what they contribute, the shameful actions they've done which make people gossip, or the beautiful, unselfish actions that no one sees. . . each person needs to know, "I am not worthless." Each life has intrinsic value, and who they are means something.

You do too. Your value exists apart from how much money you have, the shape of your body, or the features of your face, the "likes" you have on Facebook or Instagram, or the kind of work you do. The intrinsic value of people is a matter of being and discovery. Independent of the opinions and judgments of others, your value comes from what you are. That's how we all come into the world right? Not having done a single thing besides existing yet you have worth.

The rest of your life, people will have the opportunity to discover how that intrinsic value matches the needs of family, communities, and society. The human-to-human connections of family, friends, companions, coworkers, neighbors, mentors, and mentees all provide the vantage point to make that discovery and affirm the value they see in you.

Along with that external affirmation, your growth in Emotional Intelligence will help you develop stronger self-management to adjust your moods and mend pessimistic thinking. This allows you to attach your sense of personal satisfaction to internal anchors rather than being wholly dependent on external affirmation.

I sincerely hope you will find that affirmation for yourself and then make it your mission to see and affirm that in the lives of others. Please don't be content with a way of life where you isolate yourself from others. You may be the only person seeing them for who they are and providing the affirmation of their value and worth. Be willing to offer that soft rain to others and see how those actions bring refreshing and satisfaction to your own soul.

We set out to explore the valuable and lasting pieces of your life by looking at debris that ends up discarded, broken, and worthless on the side of the road. I'm sure that some of you have at points identified more with the debris than with the message in the metaphor. Please know this: every day offers a new opportunity to leave less trash on your highway. Learn what you can from the social and emotional debris of your past, and travel with better wisdom today. Slow down just a bit and take in the sights. Life isn't a race—it's a journey, and it's one that isn't meant to be taken alone.

My parting wish for you is that your road ahead be filled with wonder, discovery, purpose, and fulfilment. May you find traveling companions who bring out the best in you and are better themselves because you are traveling with them. May you notice more about yourself, your world, and the people in it. May you, through that noticing, discover ways to be at peace with yourself and others and be fully alive and content in the sights, tastes, smells, experiences, and joys you find out on the open road.

end notes

1 https://www.forbes.com/sites/lealane/2019/05/02/percentage-of-
   americans-who-never-traveled-beyond-the-state-where-they-
   were-born-a-surprise/?sh=1eb342062898

2 Taylor, James. "My Traveling Star." One Man Band, Hear Music,
   2007, Track #8

3 Tolkien, J.R.R. *The Fellowship of the Ring*. Del Ray, Reissue edition, 1986.

4 https://dot.ca.gov/news-releases/news-release-2020-014

5 Kahneman, Daniel. *Thinking, Fast and Slow*, Macmillan, 2011, p.201.

6 Seinfeld, Jerry. "Halloween." I'm Telling You for the Last Time,
   Universal, Umvd Labels, 1998, Track #5

7 NHTSA data

8 Hart, Archibald. *Depression: Coping and Caring*, Cope Publications, 1981.

9 Willard, Nancy. *Telling Time: Angels, Ancestors, And Stories*, Mariner Books, 1993.

10 Oz, Frank, dir. What About Bob? 1991, *Touchstone Pictures, Touchwood Pacific Partners 1.*

11 Franklin, R. C., & Pearn, J. H. (2011). Drowning for love: the aquatic victim-instead-of-rescuer syndrome: drowning fatalities involving those attempting to rescue a child. *Journal of paediatrics and child health, 47*(1-2), 44–47. https://doi.org/10.1111/j.1440-1754.2010.01889.x

12 Ecclesiastes 1:1-14

13 Bregman, Rutger. *Humankind—A Hopeful History*, Little, Brown and Company, 2020.

14 www.louitucker.com

15 Tan, Tay Keong. *"Silence, Sacrifice, and Shoo-Fly Pies: An Inquiry Into the Social Capital and Organizational Strategies of the Amish Community of Lancaster County, Pennsylvania"* (Ph.D. diss., Harvard University, 1998).

16 Fulghum, Robert. *It Was on Fire When I Lay Down on It.* Ivy Books, Ballantine Books publisher, 1998, p. 5.

Speaking/Teaching Engagements

Assessment and Training Services

Blogs on the Art of Peopling

Announcements on conferences
and book or product release dates

WWW.JCURTISWITT.COM

Made in the USA
Columbia, SC
12 May 2022